SHARE THE ROAD
The Journey to Autistry

Janet Lawson and Dan Swearingen

illustrations by Steven Waite

foreword by Susan Ansberry

For Ian

CONTENTS

FOREWORD

Parents of autistic children are faced with the question: how can I help my child navigate through a world that doesn't seem to have a place where they can feel happy and understood? For our family, the answer was Autistry Studios.

While Chris was in elementary school, the resources we could access through our public schools and community services seemed to be helping him progress, albeit with occasional bumps in the road. When he entered middle school, however, the strategies that had helped him when he was younger were no longer effective. As hard as middle school can be for neurotypical adolescents, it was a misery for Chris and our family. We felt there was no choice but to have him leave a general education program to attend a special needs school. This wasn't the right solution for our bright, creative child; Chris wasn't challenged, he wasn't thriving, and he wasn't happy.

It was only when we found Autistry Studios that we found a path forward. When Chris started attending the "Build Stuff" workshops, our lives changed. At Autistry Studios, Chris found friends and worked on projects based on his interests (from Star Wars to Pokémon to Egypt). Through these projects, he improved his executive functioning, fine motor, language, and social skills.

No one was happier than Chris when he was able to transition back to public school, with Autistry Studios' support on everything from study skills to using public transportation independently and, most importantly, advocating for himself at school. No one was prouder (or louder) than our family when we cheered Chris walking across the stage to get his diploma.

Graduating from high school meant that Chris was no longer eligible for services through the public school district. That would have left us in a void had not Autistry Studios launched its Autistry Comprehensive Adult Program (ACAP). ACAP helped Chris develop a plan to move into an independent adult life, including enrolling in community college to study multimedia, working in a local grocery store to gain work skills, participating in ACAP's theater arts program to improve his speech and memory (and to have fun!) and continuing to develop his independent living skills.

Thanks to Autistry Studios, we see many options ahead of Chris as he nears completion of his AA degree. Whether the next step is a four-year degree or a job that will let him develop his talents, we are looking forward to Chris living independently and pursuing his interests.

I hope that *Share the Road: The Journey to Autistry* may help others develop programs that will serve their children the way Autistry Studios has served Chris.

~ Susan Ansberry

INTRODUCTION

Welcome to a peek inside Autistry Studios. This book, Share the Road, is a compilation of notes, stories, and observations gathered over fifteen years of working with autistic teens and adults and our son. Our neurodiverse students have opened our minds to new ways of experiencing the world, and we would like to give you a glimpse of what we have learned.

This is not an academic treatise defining autism, exploring causes, or presenting the latest autism research (though there is much great work being done in that arena). Share the Road is a personal story of why and how we ended up creating a therapeutic makerspace for neurodivergent teens and adults.

The book is written in the first person plural (we, us). This can make the narrative awkward at times, but after several attempts to write in the first person or the third person we realized that these years were truly a joint effort that would be best expressed as We.

Dan is autistic. He brings his unique perspective and understanding to the work as well as his scientific, artistic, and bookkeeping skills. Janet is a born producer, and her organizational, people, and get-it-done skills helped hold the vision together and move it forward. It took the two of us working together to create Autistry Studios.

When we look around, we don't see many others doing what we're doing. Are we crazy? (The jury is still out on that!) From our vantage point, what we do always looks like the obvious direction to go. We listen to our students and follow our instincts, drawing on our own skills to help our students develop their skills.

The most common response by visitors to our program is: "I've never seen anything like this before and it is amazing!" We hadn't seen anything like it either, which is why we created it.

In the last couple of years, we have been encouraged as we see more programs supporting the strengths and interests of the neurodiverse community springing up around the globe. We want to share what we have learned with the hope that our experience will inspire others to widen their world view and create opportunities to include the visions of those who think differently.

The illustrations for each chapter are the work of Steven Waite. Steven was one of our very first Autistry students. He is now on staff. Like many of the students whose stories we tell, Steven asked that his real name be used. For those who preferred anonymity we changed their names.

We are hopeful you enjoy the stories within, and we welcome your feedback.

CHAPTER 1
LIFE CHANGES

We never expected to be the parents of an autistic child, nor would we ever have dreamed that we would one day create a program for autistic teens and adults. When we were younger, had someone asked us "What do you want to be when you grow up?" we would have answered:

"A writer." "A physicist."

"An actress." "A model railroad builder."

"A movie director." "A fighter pilot."

Like many adults, we have ended up a long way from our early notions. It would never have occurred to us that the correct answer would turn out to be "creators of innovative ways of working with autistic teens and adults and operators of a nonprofit that specializes in helping them be more independent." But, in hindsight, our personal histories include many experiences that led us in this direction and made us ideally suited to develop the program we run today.

While inventing our program might have taken special skills and experience, we feel that the processes and techniques we use are rooted in common sense and good parenting, and these can be used by any family, school, or program once the basic principles are understood. What follows is a narrative of how the program developed and how key insights came from particular personal experiences.

JANET'S JOURNEY

Far from studying child development or autism, Janet spent her twenties studying acting. She lived in Rotterdam where she co-founded a non-profit theater arts organization, wrote and performed theater pieces, led acting workshops and developed an addiction to tobacco, alcohol, and hashish. That last activity was difficult to avoid in the free-wheeling, roll-your-own world of the Netherlands of the 1970s. During those tumultuous and dramatic years, having children and being a mom were not on her agenda. But the theater work she did in those years shaped the mother and psychotherapist that she became. Even the addictions, or, more accurately, the personal struggle to overcome/manage the addictions, added a personal perspective to Janet's therapy work, allowing her to connect more deeply with those who don't quite fit society's idea of normal.

One of the first lessons Janet learned in acting workshops was that the primary task of an actor is to listen intently to the other actors on stage, to listen with your whole body to the verbal and nonverbal messages from your colleagues. She learned that to truly listen she had to silence her internal voices and restless body. A director once yelled, "Shut your toes!" as she stood barefoot on stage, wiggling her toes in anticipation of her next line. Letting go of her internal dialogue allowed her to connect to her fellow actors and to respond instinctively and naturally rather than simply following a script.

Meryl Streep once said that "acting is not about being someone different. It's finding the similarity in what is apparently different, then finding yourself in there." In that way, you become one with the character and view the world through their eyes. This way of connecting became the foundation for Janet's mothering and her practice as a therapist.

After a decade of traveling, graduating from UC Berkeley (summa cum laude), and various theater and film experiences, Janet spent her thirties getting clean and sober. She had several years of sobriety when she met Dan. In Bloomington, while Dan worked on his PhD at Indiana University (IU), Janet led Alateen meetings as part of her sobriety regimen. Alateen is an offshoot of Alcoholics Anonymous created to support young people who are affected by alcoholism in the family. The meetings are specifically set up for teenagers and are modeled after the AA 12-Step Program. Every Monday night for five years, Janet sat quietly and listened as teenagers told their stories of struggle with drug and alcohol addiction—their own and their families'. She found she loved working with teenagers. Their struggles for independence, their search for identity, and above all, their brutal honesty resonated with her.

It was her work with these teens that led her to become a therapist.

While living in Bloomington, leading Alateen meetings, working at the town library and on her Master's degree in Library and Information Science, Janet became pregnant. Towards the end of the pregnancy Janet's blood pressure started to increase and she was diagnosed with pre-eclampsia. As her due date approached, her doctors worked to induce a normal delivery. After nearly two weeks, Janet's condition deteriorated to eclampsia and Ian was delivered by emergency C-section. Ian was full term and a very healthy baby at birth.

DAN'S JOURNEY

Dan grew up in San Francisco in the 1960s and early 70s and later a bit further north in Sonoma County in the 70s and 80s. Like his father, he was always fascinated with machines and gadgets. As a teenager he learned model building, electronics, carpentry, and auto mechanics.

Dan studied physics at the local state college and joined the U.S. Marine Corps Reserve, planning to become an officer and pilot. However, at this point he suffered several years of severe failure. Looking back, Dan can now say "that's where I had the same kind of massive failure many of the students we work with today have suffered in their 20s—because I'm autistic." But he did not know that at the time. He'd had neuropsych testing in the 80s while he was in college; the results only showed remarkably uneven skills. Dan had super strong performance in some areas with amazingly poor performance in others. The modern autism diagnosis had not been developed at that time.

It was when we were researching autism after our son Ian was diagnosed that Dan finally realized that is is autistic. Dan was reading Temple Grandin's first book, *Thinking in Pictures*. Dr. Grandin is probably one of the best known autistics in the world. She has written extensively about how she experiences the world, and she describes in great detail what it is like to be a "visual thinker." A visual thinker is one who processes information through images, someone who literally thinks in pictures.

As Dan read Dr. Grandin's book, tears ran down his cheeks. "I don't know about Ian, but this book is about me." Grandin describes visualizing the design of a series of fenced pathways that guide cattle smoothly in a way that works with how cows like to move. Dan realized that this is his design process too and that he often struggles to find words to describe the extremely detailed designs he has imagined. He realized that he is a visual thinker—and autistic.

In the 80s, Dan flunked out of college, lost all rank in the service, and skirted homelessness. Frustrated but determined, he dug himself out slowly by working at a series of fast-food, retail, and blue-collar jobs. After several years Dan returned to college part-time, resuming his study of physics. At a large Thanksgiving dinner hosted by his mother, Dan met Janet.

Dan completed his undergraduate degree in Physics and also a Master's degree. Together, Dan and Janet moved to Bloomington, Indiana so Dan could work towards a Ph.D. in astrophysics. While at IU Dan taught astronomy courses and tutored local high school students in math and science. He had a reputation as a tough teacher, but his students did well, and he enjoyed figuring out ways to teach complex subjects.

Dan's Ph.D. dissertation research was developing software and processes to analyze spectra from interacting binary star systems (Doppler Tomography with Cataclysmic Variables). The dissertation work consisted of writing software that turned complex data into images that gave insight into the structure of these complex systems. He did not finish this degree. He left school ABD (All But Dissertation) and with a Master's degree in astronomy.

IN IT TOGETHER

In grad school after Ian's birth we found it much more difficult to continue financially, and Dan was starting to lose confidence he would ever be able to secure good employment as a college professor or an astrophysicist. We had done several contract projects testing early "multimedia PC" software products and writing user manuals for them. At that time, there was a new wave of tech startups using the Internet in the San Francisco Bay Area. Dan left graduate school in 1997 and immediately found work using his programming skills in this thriving arena that would later be called the Dot-Com Boom. He learned the art of translating customer ideas into workable software and quickly became

Making eye contact (Ian, age 3)

a team leader and then technical manager and manager of programmers.

IAN'S DIAGNOSIS

Back home in the San Francisco Bay Area, as the months passed, Ian continued to develop physically on track, but his speech development was noticeably below average. We had one of those "What to Expect When..." books and noted with increasing worry and dread each "normal" milestone he missed. He did not babble in a speech-like way in the early months. He was not drawn to noise-making toys, nor did he imitate different speech sounds. He seemed totally mystified by games of peek-a-boo. But he always smiled. He made eye contact. And he loved to be held. Ian seemed to communicate without words. And though we thought his utter fascination with cupboard door hinges, the pliability of a sheet of paper, or the concentric ripples in a dog's water dish was a bit eccentric, we simply chalked it up to being the son of a scientist. We took comfort in the stories that Einstein didn't speak until he was 3 years old. Even though Ian never measured up to the What to Expect When timelines, he nevertheless developed into an attractive, engaging, and affectionate child.

When Ian was two and a half years old, he dressed as the color green for his nursery school Halloween party. But first he and Janet had to make a quick trip to the pediatrician for a well-baby check and health report required by the school. At the doctor's office Ian was lost in his solitary play, enraptured by the motion of the hinges on the plastic playhouse in the waiting room. We waited a long time. Young families came, were seen, and then went. A short bespectacled man peered in periodically, watched Ian intently, and then left.

The nurse tried to record Ian's vital statistics—height, weight, eye-tracking. "He is not comfortable with strangers," Janet warned as Ian's eyes widened, his arms stiffened, and his back began to arch. To give him support and soothe him, Janet held Ian's hand while he stepped onto the scale. But the unsteadiness of the small metal platform triggered a feral response. He leapt off and burrowed into her legs, his face pressed so hard against her thighs that the seam of her jeans left an impression on his cheek.

"What if I hold him and we weigh in together. Then I will weigh in by myself, and you can jot down the difference," Janet suggested. The nurse was confused, but she agreed. When we got that sorted out, the short man with the round glasses returned. This time he beckoned us to follow. He read from a clipboard a long list of questions: When did your son first roll over, crawl, walk, speak a word, a phrase? How does he interact with others?

Janet responded honestly that Ian's physical development was right in line with the What to Expect When books. But the language development was still not there. She did not mention that she threw the What to Expect When books away as they in no way reflected Ian's growth. He developed outside their timeline—outside the norm.

Having gathered his data, a deep frown pulled at the doctor's lips, but his brown eyes softened as turned to Janet. "I believe your son is autistic."

The world stopped. Somewhere deep in the center of her mommy heart, Janet sighed with relief. This made so much sense.

She hadn't reaized until that moment just how worried she was that Ian was so much different from other children of his age. Without a reason for his difference, a name for his unique (and charming) oddness, Janet had imagined a million dire scenarios, the worst being brain damage. The fact that there was a condition called autism gave Janet hope.

The literature of the time, 1998, was beginning to reflect new thinking about autism, but the myth of the Refrigerator Mom and the Autism Bubble

Nose-kisses with Janet (Ian, age 11)

persisted. The Refrigerator Mom concept, first developed in the 1940s by the Austrian psychiatrist Leo Kanner, was an attempt to explain why autistic children seemed to live in their own worlds, often called the Autism Bubble. Much of the literature described autistic children as shying away from touch, not making eye contact, and having little interest in connecting with others.

That was not Ian. From day one he relaxed when held and he continued to seek out touch as he grew older. He would hold our fingers when walking together and he created a game of nose-kissing, rubbing his nose against ours to make a connection. But his language did not develop. His response to simple, everyday actions was often unexpected. For example, he would continue to gaze at the pointed finger rather than the object it was pointing to. We accepted that Ian was autistic.

We accepted that he was autistic.

With Ian's autism diagnosis, and seeing the huge amount of support he needed, we realized, one setback at a time, that caring for an autistic child was a full-time endeavor. Janet gave up trying to have a career and concentrated on creating a quiet, nourishing environment for Ian. As parents of autistic children know only too well, this was a round-the-clock job.

One of the first resources Janet found when researching support for autistic children was the local regional center. The social worker she spoke with recommended a pilot program that was just starting through the school district. This program was specifically for pre-school autistics ages three to six. Janet initially resisted enrolling Ian into the program. She had visions of Ian being bullied on the schoolyard or teased as he stepped off the Short Bus. Laura Wilson, the Golden Gate Regional Center social worker, persisted. "Ian needs to be around other children," she said. "You cannot do it all." And she was right.

Once he settled into the routine of saying goodbye to his mother, Ian loved going to school. With the house now quiet in the mornings, Janet was able to go back to school for another degree, this time in counseling psychology. Her goal was to learn as much as she could about how Ian's mind worked and to share this knowledge with other families to help them understand their autistic children.

As we figured out how to raise Ian, there were several key events that, in hind-sight, we see taught us very important lessons in our understanding of autism and how to support and encourage autistics.

JOINING HIS WORLD

When Ian was very young (three to four years old), he had very little language. However, he would sing songs and recite entire Disney movies word for word—especially Winnie the Pooh. He would become

Thomas the Tank Engine set arrives (Ian, age 4)

lost in this Disney world and unresponsive to any attempts to engage him or lure him into our world. During that period, he also did not sleep much at night, usually staying up playing and fussing until finally passing out asleep around 4 or 5 a.m. Dan, who had to get up early for work, needed his sleep, so when Ian crawled into their bed, Dan went to sleep in Ian's racecar bed and Janet stayed up with Ian.

One night when Ian was refusing to sleep but happily reciting lines from *Winnie the Pooh and the Blustery Day*, Janet jumped in and took the part of Tigger: "The wonderful thing about tiggers, is tiggers are wonderful things! Their tops are made out of rubber! Their bottoms are made out of springs!"

Ian whipped his head around, looked her right in the eye…and burst into laugh ter. The joy in his smile and the relief in his eyes spoke nonverbal volumes. "Mommy, you found me!" he seemed to say. Janet had entered Ian's world.

We embraced Ian's world. Watching television one day, Ian discovered the world of Thomas the Tank Engine, a bright blue steam engine with an expressive face and the star of the stop-motion animation television series, *Thomas and Friends*. Thomas has many train engine friends: Percy, Gordon, Edward and James, as well as the train cars, Annie and Clarabelle. Ian was immediately drawn to these inanimate animated characters. He responded to them in a way we had not seen before.

The simple iconic expressions of joy, sadness, and anger that were conveyed with consistent discrete details—a raised eyebrow, a down-turned mouth—clearly expressed emotions that Ian could understand. Human faces move quickly and often display conflicting expressions—a smile coupled with glaring eyes for example. For Ian, and for most autistics, these ambiguous expressions are confusing and often just ignored.

Ian soon knew every train, every person, and every word of dialogue. We bought him a train table and all the trains we could find. All. Of. Them. When we brought everything home and set it up, Ian was so excited he didn't stop playing, even to eat, for DAYS (okay, a day and a half, but it felt like forever). He would occasionally fall asleep for a nap beside the train table. Our initial excitement turned to concern. Was Ian becoming lost in the Thomas world? We reached out to therapists, behaviorists, and friends for advice. We were told to stop him and NOT to indulge this obsession. We were told to put the trains away and make Ian focus on other age-appropriate activities like riding a bicycle or climbing a tree.

However, we watched carefully and after a while, Ian resumed eating and sleeping, so we let it continue. His play with these toys remained intense, but so was the joy on our son's face. He was enraptured as he played out scenes from the TV series on his own Thomas track—and he started trying to talk. Ian would put the trains on the edge of a table facing each other and he would put his face right up to them and act out talking (well, jabbering) the interactions between characters. He was telling stories. When he went to bed, he would line up the Thomas trains on his nightstand carefully so that the trains were facing each other (so they could talk to each other). It was VERY obsessive, but our son was learning about communicating. We kept the Thomas trains, and we have never regretted this decision. He began to use more vocabulary, and his over-obsessive behaviors with the trains diminished.

Ian didn't sleep, so eventually we had to use medication to help him sleep. His pediatrician prescribed Risperidone, an anti-psychotic medication often used to treat some symptoms of schizophrenia (disorganized thinking, aggression, compulsive behavior). Risperidone may work well for some autistic children, but it certainly did not work well for Ian. He became extremely agitated, ran in circles, repeatedly banged his head against the floor, and still stayed awake most of the night. Ian was then prescribed non-stimulant ADHD medications, but those had no effect at all.

We tried more traditional remedies: small doses of Ambien and Valium. This cocktail at least soothed him enough to allow for longer periods of sleep during the night. But we worried about medicating our young son and continued to search for long-term solutions.

Ian working on the Gold Rush project (age 9)

We had started to hear rumors about how eliminating wheat and dairy from a child's diet could reduce or "cure" autism. Dan was very skeptical since there was no scientific basis for this diet. But he tried it himself for a couple of days and found it made him feel dramatically better. His energy improved, as did his ability to concentrate, and he was more easygoing. We put Ian on the diet and saw immediate improvement in his ability to regulate himself. His teachers reported that Ian's ability to participate in school and to pay attention to lessons also had improved. He started to have a normal sleep pattern, and we were able to back off all medication.

Ian's improvement at school helped him quickly learn to read. To support his reading, we turned on the closed captions on all television programs so he could read the lines that Thomas and his friends were saying. We think this helped Ian understand that reading was really talking. (He still is very good at reading aloud even when he doesn't understand all the text.) He developed a deep connection to storytelling. He would often create a circle with his stuffed animals and read to them. He even set up a library so that his animals could check out their own books. All this was at a time when his ability to communicate verbally was still very, very low. In videos from this time, Ian can be seen speaking in single words with a very small vocabulary.

Having entered and embraced our son's world, we leveraged other styles of communication. Connecting his imagination to the real world and to other people in his life created a bridge between his world and

ours. We use many of these techniques daily working with other students in our program at Autistry and call it "meeting them where they are." We go into more detail of these techniques in later chapters.

ARTHUR'S GOLD RUSH ADVENTURE

One of the greatest lessons we learned as parents was the importance of entering our child's world rather than forcing him to be in ours. Once we entered his context, we could communicate even abstract ideas and he could communicate back to us his understanding of the world. This brought rewards from unexpected places.

> ...you need to find a way into your child's world and push out from that place.

In many California elementary schools students learn about the California Gold Rush of 1849 in fourth grade. When Ian was nine years old, he was mainstreamed part-time into a regular fourth grade class. He had very low verbal ability compared to his classmates. He was still at the one- or two-word response level. The teacher and aides told us Ian was excused from any projects about the Gold Rush. They had no idea what he would be able to comprehend or accomplish. We had our doubts, too.

The Gold Rush re-imagined

The school had no expectations that Ian could do anything like the other students, but as long as Ian behaved, they were happy to have him. We were frustrated with this situation. We could tell in our communications that they thought he was sweet but not very smart.

Without language, it is extremely difficult to learn some topics. History was very hard for Ian to understand, especially in the past beyond the lifespan of any relative Ian knew. How could we teach Ian about the Gold Rush? At this time Ian loved the Arthur the Aardvark series of books and videos. We got the idea of working with Ian to make an Arthur adventure that would teach Ian about the Gold Rush. We made "Arthur's Gold Rush Adventure." We took famous gold rush photos and

Ian traced those and substituted Arthur characters for the people in the photos. Ian understood the story because he knew the characters—they were part of his world. He was very proud of his report, and the teacher loved it too. Ian got an A+.

Our goal was simply to help Ian learn something about the Gold Rush comparable to what other students in his class were learning. The completed project had some unexpected powerful positive side effects. At the next school open house, we saw other teachers, students, and parents looking at Ian's project in delight. The story reflected Ian's humor and intelligence. The most important thing Ian got out of making the story was a huge change in how other people saw him.

After this, the teachers had higher expectations for Ian and Ian worked harder to meet those expectations. His fellow students saw and appreciated our son's quirky view of the world. This work gave Ian a way to communicate his personality and abilities beyond his limited verbal capabilities.

This reinforced our conviction that you need to find a way into your child's world and push out from that place. It taught us that concise projects are excellent vehicles for learning. It also showed us that our child's work, more than his words, would establish and maintain his "personhood."

With the success of Arthur's Gold Rush Adventure, we encouraged Ian to create other projects. Dan has always been a model/miniature builder—trains, planes, automobiles, and dioramas of any topic or locale. Ian seemed to be following in his father's footsteps. He converted his Thomas the Tank Engine track pieces into highways and ran them end-to-end throughout the house. At first glance the tracks seemed random, but one day we recognized a familiar pattern. Near the dining room table, Ian had replicated the junction of Highway 580 and Highway 101 and in front of the living room sofa was the Golden Gate Bridge Toll Plaza complete with toll booths. We realized that even with a very limited vocabulary, Ian was able to retain visual information and recreate accurate topographical scenes.

DARING THE TANTRUM

If we had realized at the time how important this particular interaction

with our son was going to be, we would have done it earlier—and documented it better! By the time Ian was nine years old, he had, in a variety of ways, become a petty tyrant in our home and lives. We lived under a constant threat of a tantrum or meltdown. We had to follow an array of rituals precisely as Ian wanted—or else.

After dinner every night, Ian insisted that we turn all the lights off in the house and retire to our bedroom while he watched videos in his room. This ritual could not be altered in any way and was certainly not functional for the family, but Ian threatened to blow up into meltdown if we did not comply.

This pattern is experienced by many families with an autistic child. The signature is "I get to do what I want or I will blow up! And make you feel [choose all that apply]: embarrassed, scared, afraid the neighbors will call the police, etc."

Dan and Ian holding fingers (Ian, age 10)

After some time, we realized this was not getting better. We feared that Ian was not going to grow out of this habit. When we thought about it more, there were at least a dozen other rituals where Ian was threatening "Do what I want or I'll blow!" These rituals or habits had seemed harmless at first—lining up his toys, the same breakfast cooked the same way every morning, dinner at 5 p.m. and lights out at 9 p.m. Ian, like any smart human child, had learned to have a measure of control over his world (and his parents) by threatening an angry or uncontrolled meltdown if he did not get what he expected. All children do this to some extent, but an autistic child's meltdown is legendary, as is their stubbornness.

We had gotten ourselves into this situation by inches, having given into little demands. But over time it had grown into a real problem. After some discussion, we decided to draw the line at the after-dinner ritual. We would insist that Ian give up this ritual. We were going to Dare the Tantrum.

Why would we ever consider doing this? The biggest reason was that we felt we should not continue to teach Ian that he could control us, his school, or anyone in his life by threatening a tantrum. In the long run, it would be very destructive for Ian to be allowed to continue in this fashion. We had to firmly move things to a better, more constructive place.

We scheduled a fight with our son. For a couple nights in advance, we explained that the ritual he wanted was not helpful to Mom and Dad, and we gave him several alternatives. He was not interested in compromise.

The third night we held the line. We left the lights on! As many parents know, autistics do not bluff.

Ian blew. For an hour and a half.

Dan physically moved Ian back to his room and let him continue to tantrum. Ian was nine, so we were able to physically manage him without damage to him or to us. Ian yelled, screamed, and threw things for about 90 minutes until he was physically exhausted. We allowed him to do one of the alternative activities we had offered, and he went to bed.

The next night we stood our ground again, and this time he tantrummed for 20 minutes.

The night after that, there was no tantrum.

Within a few weeks we realized that we had crossed into a new and wonderful place with our son. Ian was happier, calmer, and more loving. Almost everything was going smoother with him. In the years since that time Ian has not had a single full power meltdown. He still complains, still yells back at us sometimes, and still can be very stubborn. But the out-of-control, the-neighbors-are-going-to-call-the-police meltdowns have been managed away.

We conclude that Ian's management of us by tantrum did not make him happier or more secure. In looking back at Ian before this intervention, we see that Ian was feeling insecure and that much of his rigidity and old behaviors were really insecurity and neediness. He was testing boundaries. Testing us.

As many researchers have found with neuro-typical (NT) children,

we strongly feel that appropriate and consistent boundaries are key to a happier and more stable child.

Appropriate boundaries mean that the rules you are imposing are not arbitrary: they follow some sort of consistent logic and the child understands them.

Consistent boundaries mean that once you have defined a boundary, you must not in any way signal that the child can overcome the boundary (overcome you) by tantrum or sheer stubbornness. Additionally, everyone in the child's life must adhere to the same boundary. We find that inconsistent boundaries across different environments and with different adults in a child's life teach children how to lie and be sneaky.

Daring the tantrum is not easy. It is painful to hear one's child screaming in seeming anguish, and there is a tremendous desire to give in and comfort the child. There is tremendous fear the neighbors will call the police. It helps to remember that this is a test and that, in order to feel safe, the child needs to feel the strength and solidity of the boundary you, as parents, provide. A child who feels safe can internalize that feeling and turn it into appropriate confidence and self-assurance.

Do this when they are still small! Now that Ian is adult size, we also realize how important it is to settle this aspect of the relationship with the child while they are still physically small. An adult-sized child with adult strength having a meltdown will often require police involvement and involuntary confinement at a medical/psychiatric facility.

Ian still pushes back when he does not agree with us and he can still be very stubborn, but he has learned to honestly negotiate with us. When we can, we work out a compromise with him. When we can't compromise, Ian has learned that he must accept our decision because he has tried to call our bluff and it didn't work.

TRAFFIC

One day when Ian was ten or eleven, we were driving one of Janet's clients home. This client was a 20-year-old medium verbal autistic woman. We got stuck in traffic, and Ian started fussing loudly and threatening a tantrum ("Don't stop! Go around!"). Our client got anxious and upset.

We realized we had grown used to his traffic behavior and now just ignored it. It took having a sensitive client in the car for us to realize that we should no longer continue to accept Ian's tantrums in traffic.

That evening we informed Ian that he had lost his computer privileges until he could behave himself when in our car in heavy traffic. He was VERY unhappy with us. But he thought about it.

The next day Dan came home from work, and Ian ran up to him and said, "Dad! We need to go find some traffic so I can get my computer back!" Dan turned around and took him out to find some heavy evening traffic. Ian sat quietly in the car the whole time. Ian got his computer privileges back and has never tantrummed in traffic since. We were happy—and shocked it had worked. The lesson to us: it is important to create a dynamic where the child practicing the desired behavior grants them the privilege they want.

Traditional punishment is based on focusing on the [bad thing]: "I will take away [thing you want] because you did [bad thing]." We have found that this mode of discipline often does not work with autistic children. It seems to make them fixate on the bad thing, fixate on what you will take away, and does little to get them to fixate on behavior that would make things better.

A child who feels safe can internalize that sense of safety and turn it into appropriate confidence and self-assuredness.

Instead, we suggest trying "You have already lost [thing you want]. Do [better behavior] for [specified amount of time] and you will get [thing you want] back." You are also saying "Use your brains and abilities to get what you want back." We have found that the child understands the implicit "if you do [bad thing] again, you will again lose [thing you want]."

Ian's ability to challenge himself to tolerate his traffic frustration encouraged us to have higher long-term expectations for him. When Ian was presented with a desired goal and given defined boundaries and appropriate support, he was able to change negative behaviors.

These experiences with Ian were the seeds from which Project-Based Therapy grew and were fundamental to the development of our Core Values.

Core Value #1: Listen to what experience teaches

CHAPTER 2
THE BIRTH OF PROJECT-BASED THERAPY

The return to the Bay Area from Indiana opened up many opportunities for our family. With his background in astrophysics and his years of experience writing software programs, Dan quickly found work in the booming Bay Area computer industry. Ian was accepted into a county pilot program for preschool autistic children and so began his public school years. Janet returned to university to pursue a Master's degree in counseling psychology and became a licensed marriage and family therapist (or, as Dan would say, "Giving up her amateur status").

Every psychotherapist in training in California is required to do 3,000 hours of combined individual client sessions, group sessions, seminars, and case note-writing. Janet did most of her client hours at local high schools, working with teenagers and their families. At that time she was one of the few therapists, either in training or fully licensed, with any experience in autism, so many of the autistic students would be referred to her.

STEVEN

One of her very first clients was a 14-year-old autistic freshman boy. Steven was highly intelligent and did well in science and mathematics. But he was not very social and reluctantly verbal. When asked a simple rhetorical social question like "How are you?" He would reply, "I am how I am." His response to "How was school today?": "It was how it was."

Steven was not rude, just economical in his responses. He also had trouble formulating complex conversational sentences, so he preferred to be concise bordering on curt. He did not want to be called out of class for counseling sessions, so he and Janet agreed to meet every Tuesday at lunch. He brought his lunch—a cheese sandwich, a small bunch

Steven's early characters – Bupim and BVG

of grapes, two cookies, and juice. He ate the same lunch every day. At first, they spent the hour quietly eating with Janet asking occasional questions that were only marginally answered by Steven.

One day Steven brought a sketch book and introduced Janet to his imaginary world. He had created several characters based on the shape of a pencil eraser—the pink rubber erasers that you can stick on the ends of pencils. Steven had created over 50 different characters—some based on a mechanical pencil, others on a pencil sharpener. He created storylines, detailed settings, and very imaginative names—often the names were puns or elaborations of words.

Janet began to see Steven differently.

The characters were stick figures, but each had a distinct personality. Steven had a definite artistic talent. He captured expression in the arch of a brow or a crooked smile. Whereas face-to-face with another person Steven seemed to lack affect, the characters in his drawings communicated volumes in subtle simple pencil lines. Janet began to see Steven differently. She looked for the subtle communication in his expressions and found that, like his characters, in his own minimalist way Steven too was reaching out. He was sharing his thoughts and emotions but with expressions that were nearly indiscernible.

Janet began to seriously take an interest in Steven's creative world, and they discussed his characters in depth. They shared online cartoons with each other. Steven had his own online comic strip which Janet followed each week so that they would have common ground to explore. Their sessions together, though never filled with the "typical" therapeutic discussions ("How does that make you feel?"), were rich with non-verbal exchanges.

Steven and Janet had lunch together every week for three years. When we started holding group sessions at the house, Steven was in the first workshop for high school aged students. At that time, Steven was a junior in high school. Fourteen years later, he still attends workshops, and he continues to develop his unique world.

GIRLS WHO LOVE ANIME

When Janet finally finished her training hours, passed the licensing tests, and hung out her Marriage and Family Therapist shingle, she con-

tinued to see autistic teens and adults. While working with a young woman, Sarah, diagnosed with what was called at that time high-functioning autism (HFA), Janet realized that trying to discuss social challenges and teen-identity issues in a small room, face-to-face, was not working. Unlike the verbose AlaTeen kids in Indiana, Sarah was not able to accurately describe problematic or triggering incidents

Peach Fairy drawn in session with Janet

and she had great difficulty describing the emotions those incidents inspired.

One day, Sarah asked if she could draw during the session. Janet quickly found a pad of paper and some colored pencils, and Sarah began to draw beautiful anime-style fairies. And she began to talk. She needed the drawing to express herself. It was as if the two channels—speech and drawing—needed to be activated simultaneously for her to fully communicate.

At that same time the parent of another young HFA woman called and asked Janet to start a group for girls. The mother was desperate. She had tried every support group from Girls Scouts to Social Skills Therapy, but her daughter, Carrie, continued to languish socially and to fail academically. Janet was reluctant to start **Many autistic individuals are attracted to anime.** a group as group sessions are generally difficult to schedule and take enormous amounts of time to prepare. But the mother was so insistent and her anguish so genuine that Janet could not say no.

During the first session Carrie sat in the office, her head down, looking at Janet over the rim of her glasses. She answered questions without elaboration and in a distracted fashion. She had obviously been through the therapy wringer and knew the drill. When Janet asked her what she liked to do most she answered, "Draw." When Janet responded that she would love to see Carrie's drawings, Carrie brought out a sketchbook. Janet expected Carrie to show some of her work, but instead she began to draw and quickly created a sketch of a young girl with large innocent eyes in a very sexy outfit.

First Autistry plushie project

Though Carrie's drawings were more sophisticated than Sarah's—and less innocent—she nevertheless seemed quite similar to Sarah, so Janet asked if they would like to form a small group. This tiny group was the starting point for the development of Project-Based Therapy and the inspiration for Autistry Studios. Every week they drew together, ate snacks, and talked. The girls drew primarily in anime style and they named the group "Girls Who Love Anime."

As they delved deeper into the subculture of anime, they discovered that Sarah and Carrie were not alone. Many autistic individuals are attracted to anime. They love the simple drawing style and find deep meaning in the restricted range of iconic emotional expressions. Many people on the spectrum often cannot decipher nuanced human facial expressions and are therefore challenged by personal non-verbal communications. In the anime world they quickly learn the simple range of expressions and their associated emotions that are used consistently across the genre. Often for the first time they start to understand emotions and their meanings in the context of narrative. They can fully participate in the communication. They can engage in the stories.

Janet wanted to challenge the girls to take their drawings to a new level. She asked them to create in three dimensions. As there was no space in her little therapy office to accommodate their creative visions, Janet invited Sarah and Carrie to her home where there was lots of

room, tools, and materials for creating projects. Sarah learned to sew by creating a plushie of her favorite character from *Super Robot Monkey Team Hyper Force Go!*

DAN AND THE NIGHT OF THE LIVING DEAD

Our project time was in the late afternoon, and Dan was often home from work at that time. As a lifelong model builder, tinkerer, and programmer, he was immediately drawn to the creative energy in the house. When Carrie asked him for help with the video editing software, Dan became an integral part of this new project-based approach to working with autistic individuals.

Carrie was very interested in Anime Music Videos (AMV). These are fan-made short music videos created from clips of an anime film synched to music. She watched these all the time but had never been able to make one herself. Dan was not (and is still not) an anime fan, but he and Carrie compromised on using footage from the original "Night of The Living Dead" (now in public domain) set to Marilyn Manson's cover of "Sweet Dreams." Their goal was to make their AMV in one fell swoop so that Carrie could experience all the steps of the project end to end.

Over the course of an afternoon, they completed the video and uploaded it to YouTube. The project was a success. Carrie loved the finished product, and this was Dan's first experience working as a mentor one-on-one. The experience would change the course of his life.

> Their creativity was inspiring even when their skills were lacking

We later realized that the key to this experience was:

1. Choosing materials easily obtained or already on hand. In the first session, it is important that external obstacles are minimal: you want to see the student's internal issues.

2. Being able to finish that first project in one sitting—a small sample sized project. The real product of the session is a working relationship that lasts beyond this one session.

3. Demanding acceptable quality. It is essential that the student be proud of their product.

The lessons we learned from these very first clients became some of the fundamental principles of Project-Based Therapy. From Steven, we learned that creating meaningful relationships with autistic individuals takes time and patience. Trust does not come easily as, generally, they are not accustomed to people understanding their world. Sarah and Carrie helped us to fully appreciate the importance of breaking out of the talk-therapy box. With them, we learned that helping a client discover their strength and develop their talents is the most effective way to support their becoming independent.

Doing projects together allowed us to experience what barriers were preventing these talented girls from being successful. We encountered executive functioning issues—the inability to make a plan and stick to it. The girls would become lost in the details and lose sight of the larger picture. We also encountered the effects of perseveration on forward progress. The girls would often become fixated on a character or a theme, and it would be difficult to move to a new project. We saw cognitive distortions such as rigid thinking, over-generalization, over-personalization, and other thought patterns that impede positive progress and social integration.

It became clear that working on projects with our clients allowed us to see, feel, understand, and experience their world in a way that sitting in a room doing "talk therapy" would never be able to do. Because Steven, Sarah, and Carrie were interested and invested in the projects, they had motivation to solve the issues that arose. As we had already found doing projects with Ian, exploring interests and working on projects with these young adults was fun and rewarding. Their creativity was inspiring even when their skills were lacking. We enjoyed it and they enjoyed it. But we did not yet have a big-picture view of this process.

THE BARN PROJECT

At about this same time, our son was finishing middle school and we were negotiating his high school placement. This evolved into a small battle with our school district. Almost all of Ian's neighbors and acquaintances from middle school were going across the street to the local high school. Ian wanted to go with them. The district wanted him to go to a more remote campus where they had focused support for "disabled"

students. We won; Ian stayed at the local high school, but it was a significant compromise. There were few services available for Ian, and he had to spend nearly all his time in a special day classroom.

Despite being in a class specifically for non-academic students, Ian was one of the only students not on track for a high school diploma. Almost all the instruction was well over his head. However, Ian successfully managed attendance and managed his behavior well. We have heard from many families that the schools often offer a stark choice: a sheltered placement where the academics are better suited to the student's ability but the social situation is isolated or, in our case, an academic

Ian graduating from high school in 2014

situation too difficult for the student but socially more fully integrated into the student community.

As Ian worked his way through high school, we realized that he would need significant support after high school. We started looking at what was available. We found that most post-high school programs were based on an assumption that by the age of 18, autistic individuals have reached their peak in both social and academic development. The programs available focused on stable care, on recreational activities, and very low-skilled part-time employment with no pay or sub-minimum wage pay. There was no expectation of continued intellectual growth and no real preparation for independence.

Touring these programs was beyond depressing. It was devastating. The artwork adorning the classroom walls was kindergarten and preschool level, and the attitude of the instructors was that anything the students produced was wonderful. There were no standards to attain, no goals to achieve. There was a feeling of suspended animation, lives on hold, and endless years of sameness to come. We were worried. Is this all there is? Is this what is left for Ian? Is this where he will be when we die?

It was our expectation and our hope that our son would continue to develop throughout his lifetime. We were not ready to accept that he would be done at the end of his high school years and would have become all that he would ever be. Our fears about Ian's future were strong. We started to explore the idea of creating something ourselves to help Ian and children like him grow into independent adults.

John's train

Janet's explorations as a therapist and the experience with the girls' group indicated a way forward. We decided to experiment, and we put together a small group of young adults that Janet knew through her practice. At the time we were living in a small apartment, so the first order of business was to find a larger space. A large house nearby with a small studio/barn in the backyard became available—it was perfect. The house also had a very large office/library space that could accommodate three workstations, a comfortable living room, and a sizeable kitchen. This combination of makerspace and home-space set the tone for our unconventional therapeutic programs.

We dubbed our new venture The Barn Project and we started our first Build Stuff Group with four students in September 2008. We let trial and error—otherwise known as "experience"—shape much of the program. Often we would try something and see what worked for the students. That was always the most important test—what worked for them. On that very first workshop in our backyard, we knew we wanted to work on projects, to build stuff with our clients—but what? We were standing together out in the barn with nowhere to sit, so the first project was to assemble shop stools. As we stumbled through this activity, we talked about what they'd like to do next. And we listened. Each student had a different passion and a different skill set. The next week we had gathered material to support each of their unique projects. Each of these projects not only gave us insight into our students but taught us lessons and techniques that we continue to use today.

John was a client Janet met at the high school where she did her psychotherapy practicum hours. John was a medium verbal autistic and loved trains. After many discussions with John, we decided to make a small railroad diorama. John had a very hard time deciding what he wanted in the diorama. We were limited to a small space: one foot by three feet. To help John identify his particular interests and to share those with us, we got a stack of photo books of local railroads. We asked John to go through the books and tag pages with Post-it notes if he found any pictures on that page interesting. He was not to dwell on why he liked the photo but to respond without thinking. Soon there were dozens of tagged pages. We photographed all the tagged pictures and printed them out as 3x5 photos. We then laid them out on the floor and arranged them into groups: trains near tunnels, water, bridges, stations, ferry boats. We asked John, "Which two groups are your favorite?" He chose tunnels and bridges. Several had both in the same picture. We put the other photos away.

From the photographs of bridges and tunnels we came up with a very simple but effective design with a single track emerging from a tunnel and crossing a small trestle bridge. We spent the next few months making this diorama in HO modelling scale (1:87 scale or 3.5mm to 1 foot), which is a very popular scale for model railroads. Everyone was very pleased with the result, and John insisted on leaving the diorama with us so we could integrate it into other Autistry model railroad projects. The train diorama became a lasting piece of the Autistry story as did the method of discovering and communicating interests that could form the foundation of a project.

Sarah expanded on the work she had done in Janet's Girls who Love Anime group. While building the workshop stools, she told us about a dream she had in which she and her dog were fly-

Sarah and her flying bed

ing in her bed above a city at night. She said it felt like Disneyland's Peter Pan's Flight. We asked Sarah to draw her vision and we all realized that this was a perfect subject for a diorama.

Sarah carefully carved pieces of pieces of wood to create her flying bed and she modified dollhouse figures to be mini-Sarah and her dog. She brought in fabric samples that closely resembled her own bedspread. We took out the sewing machine and made the spread and matching pillowcases.

For the cityscape, Sarah spray painted blocks of balsa wood and arranged them to create a nighttime profile. As we didn't have a spray booth, we built one. On one wall of the barn there was a fan that worked perfectly to draw the paint fumes away from the workspace. We used cardboard to create a large box around the fan and…voila, a spray booth was born. This became a great example of creative problem solving and a lesson for all of us that obstacles can also be opportunities.

Creating a personal project and working with one's hands can be a huge challenge, but it can also be a place of peace.

Carrie also wanted to work with her hands rather than do another music video. As a high verbal and high-strung girl, she started and discarded many ambitious projects, but a family trip to Egypt helped her settle on a diorama of an Egyptian Prince on a chariot. She built the human figures using pieces of small cast metal RPG (Role Playing Game) figures. It took several months, and Carrie had to learn to be patient and carefully build and paint the small figures. When finally completed, Carrie was very proud of the result.

Carrie's Egyptian chariot

Carrie's work on this detailed project required concentration and fine-motor discipline. The project also offered the perfect opportunity to explore self-regulating activities. We often stopped work to shake off frustration by walking around the block and did jumping jacks or other physical, large motor exercises. Frustration with the project also created openings to discuss deeper issues, look at triggering events, and explore personal experiences that were hard for her to discuss in more traditional therapeutic settings. We discovered ways for her to self-soothe by

working on less challenging portions of her project to regain confidence and control. Creating a personal project and working with one's hands can be a huge challenge, but it can also be a place of peace. Finding that balance is an important part of our program.

The fourth participant in that first Build Stuff Workshop was a young man, Paul, who, though never officially diagnosed with autism, certainly shared many traits with those on the spectrum. Paul described himself as a Hikikomori, a Japanese term for a social recluse or hermit. He was an avid, some might say addicted, online video gamer. He had attained very high levels of success in the Final Fantasy multiplayer video game. He came to the group rather reluctantly, but Janet had hoped that being in the "real world" around others who followed online games and understood the experience would provide a social opportunity for him.

In keeping with his deep interest in Japanese pop culture, he chose to build a Gundam model. In discussing this choice of a human-like robot encased in armor, we immediately saw the connection with the Hikikomori existence: social isolation, alienation. Paul had his own armor. He wore a long leather coat and a black leather hat even on the hottest of days. Though we had moments of connection with Paul as he worked on Gundam, he did not stay with the group long enough to create relationships with the other members. When Paul joined the group, he was 26 years old and had been living alone for several years. A major takeaway from our experience with Paul was that it would be best to work with autistic individuals before rigid, negative (or unhelpful) self-identity has set in. For our next workshops we lowered the entrance age to 13.

This first workshop and the ones that followed helped us identify our personal core values and those of our program. We tried various approaches, experimenting with the size of the groups and the student/mentor ratio. We did more of what seemed to work and less of what didn't. It was definitely a case of trial and error. The initial features that stood out were:

Small groups. We began with workshops of four students of roughly the same age. For financial reasons, we expanded a group to six students one semester. One would think that adding a couple of students wouldn't alter the group dynamic too much, but we found that it definitely did!

When groups are larger than five students, there are just too many possible conversation paths, too many relationship variables, and too much interpersonal "noise." The more extroverted students responded to the excess energy by over-talking, and the shyer students tended to crawl inside themselves. No one was comfortable. And our first rule was born: Workshop groups will only have four to five students.

In later years, when we added the College Support Workshop, we found that we could expand the group to six students—but only because many of the students were actively engaged with homework.

High mentor/student ratio. When a student first joins a workshop, he or she receives 1:1 mentorship. This gives us time to explore the student's interests, get to know their quirks and habits, and create a goal-based plan.

After this period, the mentor to student ratio is generally 1:1.5. This guarantees a high level of attention and interaction. The mentors are encouraged to do their own projects alongside the students, to learn with them. Relationships are the key to successful therapy and that is absolutely true for Project-Based Therapy as well.

Good cohort mix. When creating a working group, whether it be a therapy group or social group, it is essential to get the right combination of personalities and levels of sophistication. We create cohorts based on age and verbal ability. We are also very aware of behavioral issues and try to create a group that includes good peer models to help set the bar for appropriate social behavior.

Meals. One of the first things we noticed working with teenagers is that they are always hungry! In the early days we were constantly running to the refrigerator to get snacks. The importance of food became so apparent that we began to serve lunches.

At first it was just sandwiches, fruit, and chips. But the meals soon took on a more fundamental function: They became the workshop social time. Sitting around the table swapping stories and literally breaking bread together put the

We discuss table manners and expected mealtime behavior not in terms of Right or Wrong but in terms of not offending your friends or colleagues.

students at ease and created an environment within which they felt comfortable enough to share. These table discussions are now one of the main ingredients of the Autistry workshop experience.

The shared mid-day meals became more substantial over the years and now include extensive menus. We have students with many different dietary needs: gluten-free, dairy-free, vegan, vegetarian, allergic to nuts, no grains, hypoglycemic, and more. We

Lunch time around the dining table

have learned to cook meals to accommodate everyone. Cooking and dining together became a way of accepting each other's special dietary needs and normalizing what can often be a very stigmatizing situation.

Sharing meals also highlighted behaviors that could become "social-stoppers" if not addressed. We know as parents that we have to pick our battles, so we often overlook what appear to be small issues. But those small issues like chewing with your mouth open, eating messy food with your fingers, or wiping your hands on your pants instead of using a napkin can alienate a person from their social or work cohorts. We address these issues head on. We discuss table manners and expected mealtime behavior not in terms of Right or Wrong but in terms of not offending your friends or colleagues. Lunch became an opportunity to modify behaviors in order to create a comfortable group environment.

On a very practical level the meals also provided an opportunity to work together—arranging the tables, setting the table, and clearing up afterwards. We were pleased and surprised to hear from families how dinner time behaviors had changed as their child became accustomed to kitchen and dining room chores. Many families also reported increased conversation at the dinner table. Providing meals was expensive and time-consuming, but it was working so well for the students. Every time we thought "How can we afford to continue to do this?" we looked around the table and thought "How can we not!"

The early Project-Based Therapy groups taught us many lessons in what worked and what did not work. The small groups, high mentor to student ratios, meals, and individual projects are essential but resource intensive. We came to understand why other programs offered limited options to their clients—choice is expensive. But high support and individual projects are what make the groups successful.

Core Value #2: Be flexible and do what works for the client

CHAPTER 3
A PROGRAM EMERGES

Word spreads fast in the autism community. Our one Friday afternoon workshop led to many requests to add more weekly workshops. Over the next few years, we grew the program to five weekend workshops— one on Friday afternoons and two on Saturdays and Sundays. In keeping with the lessons learned in the first workshop, we kept the group size to no more than five students.

As these were four-hour workshops, we quickly amassed an enormous amount of experience, and with that came volumes of information about the many faces of autism. We began to see autism as a family of underlying key issues that support an almost bewildering menu of "developmental" issues. A metaphor we find useful is to think of autism as a type of music: jazz, classical, rock. As you train your ear, you can identify a unique song as being part of the autistic family of tunes, part of another family of tunes, or a completely new original class of tune. While it is true that every individual is different and has a different tune, you find you can learn to recognize familiar rhythms, rifts, and melodies that help you categorize individuals in useful ways, allowing you to leverage techniques that were effective with others who had a similar "tune." This is not to place defining labels on individuals but to identify tools that could help them be successful.

Autism is complex in that individuals often simultaneously have issues we think of as disabilities joined by issues we think of as mental health problems. For example, our son Ian has language processing disorder (a disability) joined by intense anxiety and occasional temper tantrums (typically seen as mental health issues). Is autism a difference (like straight versus curly hair) or a disorder or disability (like Cerebral Palsy or Down's Syndrome)? We came to think of autism as a neurological difference and a disorder.

Neurodiversity enriches the individual and the community. "Thinking outside the box" is praised as a way to find solutions that are not

obvious. Autistics live outside of the box. Student suggestions have led us to create new projects (personalized remote controlled cars, character clocks, stop-motion animation videos) and new activities (community excursions to the comic museum, exploring locations found on Google Maps). Viewing life through a different lens adds dimension to

Unconscious synchronized hair-twirling

the world. On a practical level, Ian can often find lost objects that we have overlooked because we didn't focus in on details. We can't see the trees for the forest.

As we work with more and more individuals of various ages, academic abilities, and with many different interests, we find that our students share some common fundamental issues. These fall into two groups. There are the core neurological differences and the brain differences (neural wiring or chemistry), and there are the adaptive or maladaptive responses to those differences.

PRIMARY ASPECTS OF AUTISM

The neurological differences cannot be changed. We call these the Primary Aspects of Autism. These primary aspects, or underlying autistic issues, include:

- Language development and auditory/language processing impairment
- Difficulty with self-regulation of emotion, excitement, and sensory experience
- Impaired or atypical working memory
- Gross and/or fine motor planning (dyspraxia)

Without doing a deep dive into brain neurology and the possible etiologies (which are generally as yet unknown), we will give a brief description of some of these primary aspects of autism.

The most prevalent challenge for many autistics is language, and they are often diagnosed with Language Processing Disorder. This is a serious impairment of communication. Language Processing Disorder can be expressive, the difficulty to express one's own thoughts, or it can be receptive, the difficulty to understand what others are saying. It can be both. The processing impairment often causes such delayed responses that an individual will comment on one topic when the group has moved on to another. These non sequiturs can be jarring to the flow of conversation.

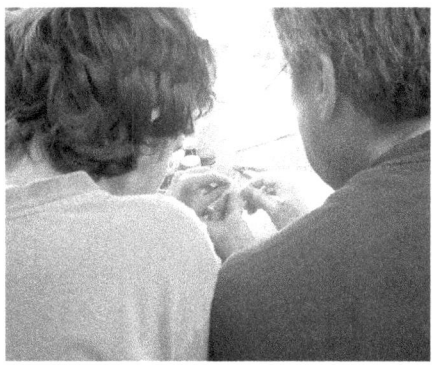

Ian and Dan sharing focus – a calming strategy

...every complete project is the wreck of a perfect design.

Another common challenge for autistics is managing high stress and strong emotions. Finding successful strategies for self-regulation is a key component of the Autistry Workshops. Being able to regulate emotional responses gives the student more control over their behavior. We help each individual find what works best for them. It may be that they need to take a break, do deep breathing exercises, go for a walk, have a snack, or discuss their feelings with a mentor in order to find emotional balance.

Jeffrey often focused so hard on his project that any misstep would cause him great anxiety. The pressure of the anxiety would drive either loud outbursts or, conversely, a total shutdown (spacing out). Dan remembered that when he joined the US Marines Corps, he was not aware of his physical response to anxiety or excitement. No one had pointed out to him that he patted his leg when concentrating and bounced on his heels when excited. Motion was, for him, an unconscious way of dealing with stimulation. Standing still had never been an option until a drill instructor screamed in his face: "You! No twitching, Marine!"

So, Dan worked out a behavioral plan with Jeffrey that included doing push-ups whenever he worked himself up into a rage or became unresponsive. After one particularly frustrating day and having done

Learning how to use the skill saw

several sets of push-ups, Jeffrey hit a snag in his railroad diorama. Without yelling or glazing over, he simply dropped down and did ten push-ups, got up, and quietly returned to work.

Another difficult emotional landscape to maneuver is one common to all creators: the finished product is never exactly what one initially envisions. Iris Murdoch once wrote, "Every book is the wreck of a perfect idea." At Autistry, every complete project is the wreck of a perfect design. Being able to reconcile the dream with the done requires emotional agility—the ability to be disappointed and yet proud of the final piece.

A difficult challenge to overcome is that of impaired working memory. Working memory is a brain function that holds different pieces of information so that they can be manipulated. We think of working memory as a workbench that can hold only a few tools. When a new tool is introduced to the full bench, in order to make room, a tool falls off the other end. This is most evident with giving instructions. Dan, who is firmly on the autism spectrum, has fabulous long-term memory storage, but when given a list of directions (turn left at the stop sign, then right onto Maple Street, follow to the end until you see a Safeway grocery store, then turn right onto Main Street), his tool bench begins to jettison tools fast. Dan will never make it to Safeway. He would be lucky to make it to Maple Street.

All projects, large ones, small ones, complex or simple, require step-by-step instructions. In the workshops, it became imperative that we take into account working memory impairments when helping our students follow instructions. We break up tasks into small sections and make short lists.

SECONDARY ASPECTS OF AUTISM

Our working hypothesis is that these core neurological differences are

the primary issues facing the ASD individual. They are parents of the constellation of issues we characterize as Autism. The issues we call the Secondary Aspects of Autism are adaptive or maladaptive behaviors acquired in response to the core neurological differences. These behaviors are learned and therefore can be treated, and significant change can be achieved. These behaviors include:

- Unsuccessful or inappropriate social interactions
- Tantrums, meltdowns, or other excessive reactions to stimuli
- Passivity and over-dependence (learned helplessness)
- Fear or avoidance of novel experiences (including new foods)

These behaviors can seriously limit an individual's ability to interact with and become a productive member of their community.

Addressing these secondary issues in a therapeutic office setting is complicated by the influence and dominance of the primary issues. Poor working memory and impaired language ability make it hard for autistic individuals to communicate the issues that are getting in their way personally,

Project-Based Therapy moves the focus away from the individual.

socially, and in the workplace. Discussing problems with a therapist can be triggering for anyone, but for someone with limited ability to regulate emotional states, the discussion can lead to strong outbursts of anger, fear, or intense sadness.

As a therapeutic method, working on projects using Project-Based Therapy moves the focus away from the individual and directs attention onto the project and on the specific goals and the roadblocks getting in the way of progress. These are generally tangible, concrete issues that can be identified and worked on without blame, embarrassment, or guilt.

Instead of staring at each other in a small room, the mentor/therapist and the student/client share a joint focus that allows for the creation of a natural, productive bond. They problem-solve together. The mentor models how to become unstuck both emotionally and practically. Over time this naturally moves to a relationship where other life issues can be discussed and worked on. Project-Based Therapy with its emphasis on a shared external focus (the project) also allows an individual the time and the physical activity to process emotions that may arise during a triggering conversation.

TRUST TAKES TIME

Before any meaningful personal information can be shared, there must be a strong, trusting relationship. We find it often takes several weeks

A moment of shared accomplishment

before a student trusts that we understand them and respect their unique reality enough for them to take the risk of letting someone into their world. The shared meals offer a great way to demonstrate that we have listened and heard them. Janet asks students what they liked to eat for lunch and then makes sure to have that food item at the next workshop. This is evidence that we not only heard them but that we thought about them during the week—an example of object permanence, knowing something is there even if you cannot see it or hear it. In this case, we let our students know that they are in our minds even when out of our presence.

Object permanence is a concept that appears in many discussions of autism. One of the early indicators of Ian's autism was his total disinterest in peek-a-boo. As he was our first and only child, we did not know what to make of this. But his grandmother, who had far more experience with toddlers, was very concerned that Ian did not engage with her in this game. Peek-a-boo is one of the first interactive activities one does with an infant. It not only reinforces the concept that an object is still there when out of sight, but it is a precursor to reciprocal social interaction and dialogue. This "peek-a-boo impairment" became apparent in other aspects of Ian's engagement with the world: toys that were put away no longer existed, chores once completed were done forever, and people whom he didn't see regularly could not be relied upon and were therefore not part of his world. Understanding the dynamics of peek-a-boo helped us to truly understand the importance of consistency when developing rapport with our students. As we added staff to our program

we emphasized being on time and showing up regularly.

Our little experiment was working. The program we started was fun for the students and fun for us, and the response from our early families was overwhelmingly positive. In the beginning, we did everything ourselves. We led the workshops, met with families, did the record keeping and the financial tracking, mopped the floors, and cooked the lunches. At this **...we realized we needed help!** point Dan still worked at his day job but twisted his hours so he could take Friday afternoons off to help with the workshop. But when we added a third weekly class, we realized we needed help. We needed staff—not full time yet but help a few afternoons a week. As anyone who runs a small business can tell you, this is a big step.

Our first hires were Nate Yates and A.J. Kaur. Nate was Ian's middle school special education teacher. A.J. was a Marital and Family Therapy (MFT) intern whom Janet knew from when she worked as an MFT Intern at San Rafael High School. Nate and A.J. set the standard we have continued to require for our staff: bright, energetic, creative, well educated, and most of all, great at working with our students.

Mentor and student research together

Besides having more hands to do things, adding staff had a powerful unanticipated side effect: our new staff could watch what we did and tell us what we were doing. The obvious question is: "Why didn't you know what you were doing?"

The answer is, as Nate and A.J. quickly pointed out to us, our working method with our students is deeply rooted in our approach as parents, and much of it is automatic responses that we make unconsciously. This made it essential that someone besides us was watching and reporting what we did. We usually knew what effect we had, but we were amazingly hazy on what we did to get that effect.

To some extent, that is still true to today. Over the years we hosted many occupational therapists and social work interns. They have helped us define our strategies and interventions and place them in the context of therapeutic disciplines. One of the goals of this book is to present how our process developed. We are also creating a manual for other communities to use. For too many years much of this information has been buried in our heads.

BUSTING THE BRAIN

One of our first realizations was the importance of challenging the habits, assumptions, fears, and ingrained resistance of our students. It is often said that there is no one more stubborn than an autistic. We can certainly agree with that. But finding a way to challenge someone in a respectful, kind, and caring, yet effective way is a challenge in itself. Temple Grandin refers to this effort as the Loving Push. We call it Busting the Brain.

Change must be experienced, not just imagined. As a young boy, Ian had a fear of rain. He would refuse to go outside even with an umbrella, boots, and a waterproof jacket. One rainy day we decided that we would no longer be held hostage by Ian's fears. It was time to challenge those fears. The weather was wet but not stormy—enough rain and wind to raise his fears but not so dramatic that it was traumatic. Janet drove Dan and Ian a mile or so from the house and let them off. There was no way home but to walk through the rain. At first Ian threw a tantrum, stomping his feet and screaming. But, since there really was no alternative, he began to trudge toward home. As he walked, his anger and frustration dissipated. He began to splash through the puddles and enjoy himself. He literally walked through his fear. Rain is no longer an issue for him. He had successfully busted through the barrier in his brain that had prevented him from enjoying the simple pleasure of walking in the rain.

Fear of rain is no longer an issue

The success of the Challenge the Rain experiment with Ian led us to reevaluate our expectations of his ability to learn, to adapt, and to change. It also changed our way of viewing other autistics. Pushing students to do their best became a key component of our approach to working with ASD individuals. It is our deep belief that they are far more capable than they have been allowed to express. With that in mind, we expect and insist upon the highest quality work they can achieve.

THE BIG PUSH

Many of our students come to us from programs that applaud any artwork or any accomplishment with equal enthusiasm regardless of the quality. As parents who put every drawing, painting, or verse on the refrigerator door, we understand this. But as professionals working with young adult and

Not all attempts are successful

adult clients who are searching for their place in the world, this unconditional accolade is not helpful. If all attempts are treated equally, then there is no incentive to reach higher.

Jennifer came to Autistry with definite talent and a strong drive to create. She built chairs out of cardboard, painted in fine detail, and was a master of the sewing machine. She produced in abundance, but the quality of her finished pieces did not reflect her ability. When we first pointed out to her that her work was uneven, polished in some places and sloppy in others, she was surprised. No one had ever questioned her work or looked at it with a critical eye.

"Just because you're autistic doesn't mean you can get away with sloppy work," we told her. Jennifer rose to meet the challenge. She took direction and learned to view her work critically to catch errors. The overwhelmingly positive response to her new work gave her the confidence to take on more complex projects.

We have found that if we set the bar high enough—not so high that the goal is unattainable but high enough that it is a stretch—our students will meet or even exceed our expectations. An honest assessment of a student's work shows respect for the individual.

DON'T CHEAP OUT ON STAFF

People often ask us why we don't use volunteers to keep our payroll costs down. It sounds like a great idea, but in practice we have found that our students do not form strong relationships with mentors who attend workshops irregularly. This is another indication of how important relationships are to the success of the program. The bond between an Autistry mentor and client is unique. It is a bit like an apprentice with a master craftsperson.

The mentor is also available as a sounding board

But, unlike the apprentice/master craftsman relationship, our mentors tend to learn with our students rather than teach them. Often the mentor does not know how to build the project the student wants to create, so together they research, experiment, and learn the necessary techniques. In that way, the mentor and the student are peers, both exploring outside their areas of comfort and familiarity. The mentor is also available as a sounding board, someone with whom to share problems and successes. In that way, the mentor is like an older sibling.

It takes time and consistency to build the trust needed to share personal information. The very few volunteers we do have at Autistry must commit to regular workshop attendance over at least one semester. Anything less and the volunteer never gains entry into the client's world. We staff with highly qualified mentors, give

Figuring next steps in making body armor

them health insurance, feed them, and pay them a competitive wage. Why? Because Autistry Workshops are not custodial programs. If our goal were merely to keep students safe, we could have larger groups, employ less qualified staff and fewer of them—just the minimum necessary to ensure safety. However, our standards are much higher. We've determined that small groups, 3-6 students and 2-5 staff (nearly 1:1 staffing)

are required at each workshop to support the progress we expect. And in most cases, progress is made.

Project-Based Therapy, using the shared experience of creating unique projects to build a strong, trusting relationship and explore individual possibilities, is an extremely effective approach to working with neurodiverse individuals—or, in fact, any individual. This strong trust allows the student to take risks they would never have taken, to challenge themselves to reach further than they ever thought they could—and much further than anyone expected of them.

Core Value #3: Neurological differences may define us, but they need not limit us

CHAPTER 4

LAUNCHING

When we added our fifth workshop in the backyard barn, it became apparent that the situation was not sustainable. The space was too small, so activities naturally spilled over into our house. Our living room floor was used for sorting materials. The kitchen became a science lab where high school students practiced their homework projects. What had been our office was turned into a high-tech computer lab with several desktop computers and laptops on every surface. After several months, the wear and tear on the house was just too much. Added to that, the city would not give us a busi-

The office in full use

ness permit to run a pre-vocational program for autistic teens and adults in a residential area. The neighbors didn't complain. In fact, they would drop in to see what we were creating. But we had to move.

We searched for several months and one day found a listing for a 10,000 square foot warehouse. When we opened the metal roll-up doors, we saw a huge open space filled with possibility. What most of our friends saw was a cold, noisy, and expensive old building on a dead-end road surrounded by auto repair shops. Our Board of Directors, our friends, and even our biggest supporters thought we were crazy. But we held fast to our vision and signed a five-year lease.

Empty space, ready for us!

LEAVING THE BARN

This was more than a change of location. It was a life-changing commitment. We had seen the power of the workshops and we were both fully invested—heart, soul, and wallet—in exploring and expanding this experiment. Dan left his Director of Engineering job. Janet gave up her therapy office. We were now full-time employees of what we called Autistry Studios: the Therapeutic Makerspace.

The larger space allowed us to accept more individuals into the workshops. The new students were no longer just coming from Janet's private practice and therefore well known to her. These new students were being referred by other clinicians or schools or from other Autistry

Moving day

families. We soon realized the importance of a thorough intake process.

We discovered there are several dynamics in play and that it is essential to actually meet the prospective student, even if there has been a long phone call with the parents, even if the parent sends stacks of neuro-psych reports and test results. We find that often parents are anxious and try to avoid having us meet their children. They are afraid we will meet their child and say NO and yet another hope for help will be dashed. But an in-person meeting with the student is a must.

Many families have experienced years of judgment and rejection by community programs and are understandably reluctant to go through the process. They have often also had the experience of their child rejecting a program, either initially refusing to attend or attending and then having a serious meltdown in order to be thrown out. As we had discovered, it is difficult to find a program that supports intellectual growth, challenges an individual, and provides the emotional and practical scaffolding needed for their success. And it is very difficult to find

a program that the individual enjoys and that meets their needs. It is important to note here that regardless of the student's age, the parents are almost always in the picture to some degree. We do in-depth phone interviews or in-person interviews with the family before we meet the prospective student.

There are many reasons we feel it necessary to meet the students before committing to working with them. One reason is that parents often do not completely (or accurately) describe their child. As parents we understand this; of course, we describe our son at his best to others. When we meet a new student, we always look for their strengths and interests. We know how bad it feels when your child is rejected or fails because people see only their disability, not their ability.

> **When we meet a new student, we always look for their strengths and interests.**

Another consideration is that the new student would be joining an existing group. Protecting a current cohort of students is a higher priority than accepting a new student with unknown issues. Our workshops are small, no more than six students, so any one student can have a great impact on the dynamic of the group. Having students join and then leave a group or attend sporadically creates anxiety. "Where is John? Why isn't he here? Is he coming back?" We would field endless questions from the students who feel the disruption to the group dynamic. A missing student is a change and, as we say at Autistry:

CHANGE SUCKS!

Many autistics are shy. They rarely like to go someplace new; they worry about who they will have to meet. We want to see prospective students at their best. To minimize stress, we invite prospective stu-

Celebrating a birthday

dents to tour the studio when it is empty of staff and students. We have tried conducting intakes with other students and staff around. It was immediately disastrous. The presence of other people prohibited the new student from exploring the studio, and it also disrupted the workshop group.

We learn a lot from observing: what in the studio grabs the student's attention—the tools, the books, the projects, the computers? Some individuals are immediately drawn to the creative dioramas, others go directly to the remote controlled cars or the many power tools.

When Ian was given his official diagnosis of autism at age three by Dr. Bryna Siegel, we asked her what her first hint was that he was autistic. "He ran straight for the toy trains in my office. He was not interested in the dolls, books, or other toys." This was reminiscent of the pediatrician watching Ian study the hinges on the waiting room playhouse. The lesson we learned from that: Observation reveals more than an interview.

As difficult as it is to say no to a prospective student, we have learned to respect an unsuccessful intake. An unsuccessful intake means our program will not be helpful for this student. A problem for us is that we are by nature problem-solvers. We want to "make it work," and initially we accepted many students who displayed problematic behavior during the intake because we were sure we could solve all problems and make it work. It never worked out. It was **always** the wrong move. We learned that unless it feels really good during the intake, and it is an obvious yes, it is not a good idea to proceed.

RED FLAG: STOP

Here are two examples of unsuccessful or marginally successful intakes:

Problem: The grumpy student. If the prospect goes through the whole intake with a hostile attitude and is silent or only says negative things, it's a bad intake. Very often the parents will be working hard to keep the conversation going and try to keep it friendly, but the intake is for the student, not the parents. We've never succeeded in our group program with a student who was seriously grumpy during the intake. We allow a second chance, a second full intake if it was just a bad day, but it has been rare that a student turns it around. We have had students return years later when they, not their parents, decided they want a change. At that point they are ready for a challenging program.

Problem: Student with poor impulse control. "Autistics with Power Tools" is one of our taglines. And though it is what we do, it also presents risk. We have a shop filled with sharp hand tools and every maker's dream collection of power tools: band saws, table saws, chop saws, CNC routers, nail guns, drills, and many, many more. We have tons of useful but toxic chemicals. Most people, neurodiverse and neurotypical alike, have an innate respect for objects that can do serious personal harm. We tend to be cautious around large trucks or powerful lawn mowers. We think twice about diving into the waves when the surf is pounding heavily against the shore. But for some people that caution is overridden by a strong impulsive desire to touch the dangerous object or be engulfed by the swirling chaotic waters.

> **...martial arts training can be a very effective means to understanding and learning how to control one's emotionally triggered behaviors.**

Chaz, a 13 year old boy, came to his Autistry tour filled with excitement and enthusiasm. He was immediately drawn to the dioramas that contained animal or human figures. He ran from one diorama to the next. But even with several firm directives, he could not keep himself from touching the figurines. Though his intentions were not destructive, his touch was not gentle. In a very short time, he had broken several clay figurines. When we spoke with Chaz and his parents after the tour, we all decided that he was not ready yet to join a workshop. His interest was great, his desire was great, but his impulse control was out of control. We recommended that they focus on self-regulation. We discussed several options.

Ian tests for his yellow belt

The one he was most interested in was martial arts training. The discipline, regularity, and clarity of expectations in martial arts training can be a very effective means to understanding and learning how to control one's emotionally triggered behaviors. Chaz returned to

Autistry two years later, at age 15 and successfully joined a workshop.

Major red flags are pretty easy to see. The major red flags in the intake process are when the parent is interested but not the student and when the student has severely poor impulse control. But some intakes are not an immediate yes or no. These are more like yellow flags highlighting concerns rather than show-stopping problems.

YELLOW FLAG: PROCEED WITH CAUTION

Concern: The student pays attention to the staff and ignores the studio. This can appear to be a good intake, but our studio is set up as an "autistic stimulation device." Autistics normally get excited by what they see at the studio. When a prospect ignores the studio and only wants to engage with staff, it can be a hint that something other than autism may be in play. Individuals with intellectual impairment often behave this way in an intake since they generally have near normal language and social skills.

It can be surprising how different autistics are socially compared to other populations. Our son was in an early intervention pilot program for autistics at age three. We often visited the classroom and stood at the door. Ian might see us and wander over, but the other autistic children would generally ignore us.

Next door was a classroom for three-year-old children with Down Syndrome. When we stood in that doorway, all the kids would come over and ask us who we were. They would introduce themselves, tell us about what they were doing, and ask whether we would be playing with them. We were stunned by the difference in language and social skills.

At first, we limited our student body to those with autism (with or without a formal diagnosis). But over the years we have learned and broadened our scope to include students with communication, social, and life skills challenges regardless of autism—as long as the student is ready for a challenge, has a true desire to move forward, and would benefit from what we do in the program.

Concern: The student was a good intake, but the family not so much. Our most successful engagements span many years. The student is the priority, but the family is in our program too. They have a huge role. If the family displays disturbing or uncomfortable behavior, they could be difficult later.

Family behaviors that are disturbing include talking over the student or contradicting the student's description of themselves or a description of an event. This is generally an indication that the family has not accepted that their child has a distinct and rather different reality from theirs. This becomes a problem with goal setting as the family may have decided that given their son or daughter's math ability, they are destined to be actuaries. But the math skill may be an inherent ability to process numbers, while the student may have no real interest in math or even a full understanding of the higher principles of math itself.

We must confess to having this same dilemma with our son Ian. He is very physically coordinated, so we naturally figured he would love to play sports. We took him to a great local sports program for "special needs" kids. He was fabulous at baseball. He could throw, hit, catch, run—all the basic requirements of the sport. But when asked if would like to return the next week, he said no. When we delved a bit further, we realized that Ian did not understand the competitive nature of the game. For him it all came so easily: ball comes toward you, you catch it. If you have a bat, you hit it. The actual running the bases to score points had no appeal for him. In fact, after hitting the ball into the outfield, he would stop and talk to the other players instead of running the bases.

As easy as throwing a ball

Neither of these issues, the hyperfocus of the potential student on staff rather than projects or the behavior of their family, would be reasons not to accept an individual into the program. We work with the families to help them understand and accept that their child experiences the world differently. We help them let go of expectations based on assumptions. The Autistry program is as challenging for the families as it is for the student.

HIRING UNKNOWNS

As our student body grew, so did our need for staff. Just as we had to develop an intake process for the students, we needed to design an interview process for new hires. But how to assess whether a person would fit well into this unique neurodiverse environment?

> We help them let go of expectations based on assumptions

We looked at who had worked best with our son. When Ian was very young, we had hired babysitters either from the local college (Indiana University) or from Janet's workplace, the Monroe County Public Library. One of his favorites was Emily, a music major at the IU School of Music. She played violin and she shared that passion with Ian. He followed her finger movements with total focus. They formed a very special bond based on wordless communication. His face lit up whenever Emily came through the door.

Years later, Emily's son was born with a rare birth defect, agenesis of the corpus callosum (ACC). ACC is an absence of transverse fibers that connect the two hemispheres of the brain. Many individuals with ACC share issues common to autistics, including difficulties with communication and social interaction and challenges with self-regulation. Emily's experience with Ian was a good foundation for parenting a neurodiverse child. And Ian's experience with Emily gave us a picture of the power of nonverbal communication and the importance of sharing one's passion.

As we interview mentor candidates, we of course ask about job history, education, and all the usual background questions. But we also ask about hobbies and personal interests. We look and listen for that personal passion. Because of this we have hired some amazingly talented and gloriously diverse mentors.

OUT OF GAS AND GOAT POOP

One of our first hires at the warehouse studio was Sara Gardner. Sara arrived casually dressed in slightly mismatched attire. She had a great résumé with years of experience working with young autistic children. She was also beginning her master's program in counseling psychology with the aim of becoming a psychotherapist. What set her apart from other applicants was her love of horses, her musical ability, and

her desire to bring both of these passions to her work with autistics. In the interview, Sara did not quote statistics or theories. She talked about what she had learned from giving riding and music lessons to autistic children. We hired her without reservation. That her car had run out of gas and she asked to borrow some money to fill the tank only added to her charm.

Over ten years later, Sara is now a licensed psychotherapist and the Clinical Director of Autistry. In addition to working with the students in project-based therapy workshops, Sara manages the equestrian program we have created in collaboration with Square Peg Foundation. The Square Peg program (which we will describe in a later chapter) provides retired thoroughbred horses sanctuary and provides autistic youth and adults the opportunity to care for them.

Sara Gardner with Skiff

One of the most memorable interview encounters was with a young person who had been recommended to us by a local college's special education program. Courtenay (they/them) had excellent references and all the right qualifications: creative, bright, and a good sense of humor. The interview was proceeding well when they became quiet, then looked up and asked "Have you ever thought about how goat poop pellets are made? Do they form as pellets in the stomach or in the intestines—or are they cut into small pieces as they exit the butt?" For many people that would have been the end of the interview. But we both laughed and actually thought about the digestive process of goats. We asked Courtenay what had led them to this question. They described a thought process not unlike that of many of our students. We had been discussing the risk of power tools, which reminded them of slicing food for their mother's pet goats, which reminded them of goat poop. Like many of our students, they shared the end result without considering their audience. No filter. It was simply a thought they had, and they were sharing it. We hired them. Because of their genuine authenticity and guilelessness, the

Autistry students immediately trusted Courtenay. They felt Courtenay understood them.

One of the common questions we get from mentors after they have been with us for a few months is "Do you think I'm on the spectrum?" And very often they are. Some staff require almost as much support as the students. We call those individuals "clienteers." They are volunteers or staff who, in many ways, would benefit from being a client in the program because they lack executive function skills or social skills. The lack of these skills causes occasional awkwardness but can be balanced with peer staff support. Several of our staff have autistic siblings or even autistic twins. They have grown up with an autistic individual and understand and accept them in a way that inexperienced neurotypicals rarely can.

After several years of hit and miss hiring, we developed an interview process not unlike the intake process for our students. We do an initial phone interview to answer questions and to gauge interest. Then we do an in-person interview at the studio at a time when no students or staff are present. That interview is more in-depth and allows for more time to ask questions and get to know each other. Like with the intake, we do a tour of the studio to see what projects, tools, or displays draw the interest of the prospective mentor. If after that interview, we are all comfortable going forward, we ask the applicant to attend two workshops to see if there is a natural fit with the other staff and with the students. Just like with the potential student, we learn more about the mentor applicant from observing them than by interviewing them.

In his essay *Mentoring: Seven Roles and Some Specifics,* Martin J. Tobin provides a wonderful etymology and definition of the term mentor:

> In Homer's legend, when Ulysses, the king of Ithaca, went away to make war on the Trojans, he left his infant son, Telemachus, in the hands of Mentor. Ulysses was gone for twenty years, and Mentor guided Telemachus in practical skills, such as archery and wrestling, and also provided advice on moral matters. Giving advice, however, is naive and presumptuous. Naive, because experience cannot be transmitted; instead, each generation has to acquire it for itself.

> Presumptuous, because no one has a monopoly on wisdom; and those imagining themselves well-endowed are the least wise.

The quality we look for in a mentor is primarily a willingness to learn new things. We have found that the most powerful way to teach is to learn with the student. We are often faced with questions that we do not have the answers for. We do not pretend to know the answers. We research with the student to find the solution and then together we explore and experiment to see if that solution actually solves the problem. In this way we model how to learn rather than simply teach.

We live in an area with several universities and community colleges nearby. These institutions are a wonderful resource for interns. The student interns are generally pursuing master level degrees in counseling psychology, social work, or occupational therapy (OT). Of the three disciplines the OTs are the most effective mentors for our students. OT interns have a coaching rather than curing perspective. They study how to help individuals strengthen their abilities. Many autistics receive occupational therapy sessions when they are in elementary school to overcome handwriting problems or basic motor planning issues. Motor planning is the process of executing a desired movement. The process relies on the individual's ability to remember a series of physical actions such that the motion becomes automatic—like brushing one's teeth or tying one's shoes.

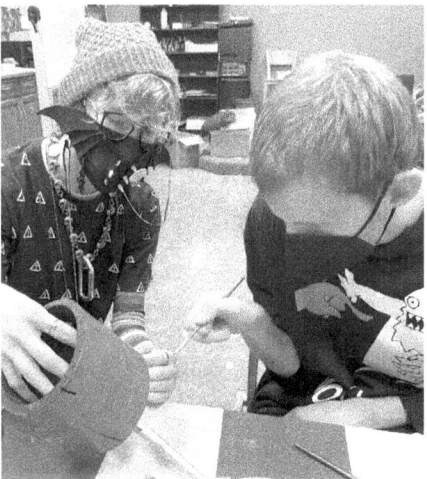

Benji Harrington helping with fine motor activity

Occupational therapy services tend to drop away as a student gets older. Our Project-Based Therapy involves fine motor skills in activities that a student may not have engaged in before—for example, using a ruler or compass, cutting with sharp scissors or saws, soldering wires together, or navigating a bandsaw. The OT interns work 1:1 with our students to help them overcome any issues when creating their projects. They also teach us new strategies and provide us with a new way of viewing physical or planning obstacles. They bring their passion to our process and we all benefit. Several OT interns have become valued staff members at Autistry.

Over the years we have had many passionate, creative professionals with specific skills (woodworking, poetry, welding) apply for positions at Autistry. Those that are hired are those who can see beyond their own special talents and join with the students to explore the unique worlds of autistic individuals.

Core Value #4: Share your passion and be willing to learn

CHAPTER 5

THE PROJECTS

At the heart of Autistry Project-Based Therapy are the projects. Each project begins with an exploration of interests and progresses through a series of steps leading to a finished product. Having identified a topic, the next step is to wrestle the first big idea into a manageable project size—in other words, scoping. This requires negotiation and, ultimately, an acceptance of what is possible. Mentors help the students navigate the inevitable emotions as fabulous visions are transformed into real-world possibilities. The projects provide a focus and a tangible goal shared by

Autistry looks like a crafts program. But it is not.

Power sanding!

the mentor and the student. The goal is to create a project, and that requires overcoming the many obstacles along the way. As the project is the vision of the student, there is buy-in to solve the problems that can be technical as well as personal.

From the student's perspective, Autistry is all about the project, the creation of a diorama, video, or model that they have wanted to make. From the mentor's perspective, Autistry is all about the student. It is about helping them learn about themselves, overcome anxieties, and find a way of being that allows them to be productive. From the outsider's perspective, Autistry looks like a crafts program. But it is not. The arts and crafts aspect of the program is actually a lure to attract and engage clients while they take steps toward independence and hone their social skills, workplace etiquette, communication, and, primarily, their executive function skills.

Executive function is a term used to describe a group of cognitive processes that regulate, control, and manage other cognitive processes. These include:

- Inhibition (filtering out superfluous input)
- Initiation and monitoring of actions
- Mental flexibility (ability to hold and compare differing views)
- Paying attention
- Planning
- Problem solving
- Task switching
- Verbal reasoning

BUILDING STUFF

These processes are needed to build things. Creating projects, in the way we do them at Autistry, supports the development of executive function in a

Award winning mixed media SeaScape

very direct but not obvious way. The early workshops taught us that planning was essential to producing quality outcomes. Autistry projects are thoughtful rather than cathartic or mindless pastimes. We remembered the artwork we had seen on the walls when touring other programs in search of support for Ian. Those sad pieces reflected no thought, no design, no passion, and no skill. We decided that we would challenge our students to push themselves to create at the highest level they could attain and improve their skills to better express themselves.

NO MACARONI ART

"No Macaroni Art" became our mantra. No art with no thought. No art with no planning. On crazy days when we find ourselves elbow-deep in silicone gel or chasing down that perfect, teal-colored feather, No

Macaroni Art reminds us there is a higher purpose to all these wonderful projects. No matter what bizarre constructions are taking shape on the shop floor, we know there is an underlying therapeutic and learning process at work.

> There is a higher purpose to all these wonderful projects.

Projects are a big part of why a student wants to come to Autistry, and we respect that by working very hard to accommodate as wide a range of projects as possible. In general, the only projects we avoid are those that are physically too large and expensive or require heavy machinery, welding, and foundry work. We have also found that autistics often have a narrow but intense area of interest. When we work on projects within their personal interests, the work is fun and very rewarding. This can lead to some very interesting projects.

DINING WITH RUSH LIMBAUGH

Andrew is a medium verbal autistic who is obsessed with politics. Andrew had discovered the conservative talk show host Rush Limbaugh's radio show and thought Rush was the funniest man alive. We were challenged to find a way to incorporate Rush Limbaugh into a project.

Rush Limbaugh puppet with meds

After several discussion sessions we all agreed that Andrew's motivating interest was the outlandish things that Limbaugh said. Andrew came up with the idea of creating a Rush Limbaugh hand-puppet that he could use to impersonate the controversial pundit. The creation of the puppet provided many opportunities to strengthen Andrew's executive function skills. Before diving into fabric with a sharp pair of scissors or molding a piece of sculpting clay, Andrew needed to have a clear idea of what the puppet would look like. That took planning. He spent hours researching. He gathered photos of Limbaugh, sketched the puppet, and even found a tie from the Rush Limbaugh Collection. With the help of the Autistry mentors, Andrew finished his puppet by adding salient details: a cigar glued to one hand and a bottle of OxyContin glued to the other. The puppet was an immediate hit at Autistry.

Andrew likes making projects that make people laugh when they see them. For his next project, he wanted to build a model out of wood. He was drawn to the photos of thematic roadside diners and motels shaped like hot dogs, animals, or pianos that he found in Jim Heimann's book, *California Crazy and Beyond: Roadside Vernacular Architecture*. Continuing the previous theme, Andrew and the Autistry team designed the Rush Limbaugh Diner.

The Rush Limbaugh Diner was in many ways the perfect Autistry project. It offered several opportunities for the students to learn new construction skills by using various hand and power tools, accurate-

ly measuring, and carefully assembling. Built in 1:12 scale (one inch to one foot dollhouse scale), it was a whimsical storybook style building attached to a huge bust of Rush Limbaugh. It combined Andrew's passionate interest and his desire to work with wood. While working with Alan on his projects, we learned the importance

Rush Limbaugh Diner - all you can eat!

and great impact of exploring, without judgment, our student's interests. Without truly listening to Andrew, not one of us at Autistry would have ever thought to create the Rush Limbaugh Diner.

SCOPING

Darren was a high-verbal man just graduating from high school who came to Autistry wanting to build a tank. A real tank, a full-size M-3 Stuart—14 feet by 8 feet, weighing 32,400 lbs.

Darren had difficulty grasping that it was not possible to forge, cast, and machine 16 tons of steel in our little backyard. After much negotiating, we agreed on a model tank. The life **Scale your projects to your abilities and to available resources.**

lesson he learned was how to scale your projects to your abilities and to available resources. Darren built several WWII tank models and went

on to create replica vintage weapons. He also managed a realistic pathway for post-high school education: two years at a local community college to complete his general education requirements and to learn how to be a college student. With those skills and achievements under his belt he went on to graduate with a B.S. degree from a four-year college. At last report Darren had completed a Master's degree in History.

SUICIDAL EGGS

The projects also opened up new opportunities for creative exploration and skill building for our son. At that time, Ian loved (and still loves) to watch YouTube videos, especially humorous ones. One of his favorites was a stop-motion animation featuring a carton of eggs who are dismayed to find they are going to be cracked open, dropped into a frying pan, and eaten. We helped Ian make his own version of this story.

The act of drawing the storyboards helps to lessen anxiety.

He began by creating a storyboard. We printed out several pages of storyboard templates that are basically a few rows of blank boxes with lines for adding comments. We asked Ian to draw simple line sketches of the important story points. Highlighting these informative moments helped him understand the arc of the narrative. The eggs in a carton on the countertop with surprised expressions drawn on them, close ups of individual eggs as they "speak" to each other, the close-up shot of the frying pan to build suspense, a suicidal egg

Frame from Screaming Eggs video

poised on the edge of the carton, and that same egg lying broken on the kitchen floor all told a story of desperation that Ian could understand.

There are several comic book creation software programs available that allow you to drop in photos or drawings and add dialogue bubbles. These programs work well for creating storyboards. But often the process of actually drawing the story elements produces a deeper understanding of the story and helps develop perceptual skills. The physical act of putting pencil to paper (or paintbrush to canvas) helps prepare the brain for deeper reflection by focusing one's attention and eye-hand coordination on a single point. We also found that the act of drawing the storyboards helps to lessen anxiety about the project by providing concrete representations of mental images. The storyboard functions much like a daily To Do List that takes the angst out of swirling thoughts.

Having made the storyboard, Ian began shooting the video. He enlisted another Autistry student as his star actor. They shot the video in our kitchen. Ian and his mentor, Nate Yates, recorded the voiceover with Ian providing all the voices. The process of editing provided another great skill building opportunity. Ian learned to use editing software, importing the sound files and syncing up the visuals. The video has become an Autistry favorite, and Ian's Screaming Eggs, as of this writing, has 103,431 views on YouTube.

Ian's next project was a diorama of a classic dojo based on his local tae kwon do dojo. Ian made a class of tiny participants out of wire armatures and polymer clay. These characters were a challenge for his

Ian's dojo diorama

fine motor skills, but with practice and continued focus he became quite good at manipulating the clay.

The surprising takeaway for us on this project was Ian's insistence that the diorama include, what for him, were the essential elements of the space: the portrait of the Master-Teacher and the bathroom doors.

A key ingredient to successfully complete a project is the ability to maintain self-control. Janet recalls the many times throughout her life, from the high school classroom to the Hollywood film set, when professors/directors had told her "The only thing stopping you is you." After years of working with the students on often frustrating projects, she finally understood that advice.

> The only thing stopping you is you.

Working on projects can also be personally revealing. Engaging in deep personal conversations with a therapist one-on-one in a small office can be overwhelming for an autistic (or for anyone). The office dynamic often feels confrontational rather than supportive. Working side-by-side on a project and sharing a joint focus is less anxiety producing. The shared project experience is like standing next to your grandmother washing dishes at the kitchen sink. As you take the warm, wet plate from her and begin to dry it, you are more comfortable sharing your worries and your dreams. Grandma is not staring at you, waiting for a response to a difficult question like, "How does that make you feel?"

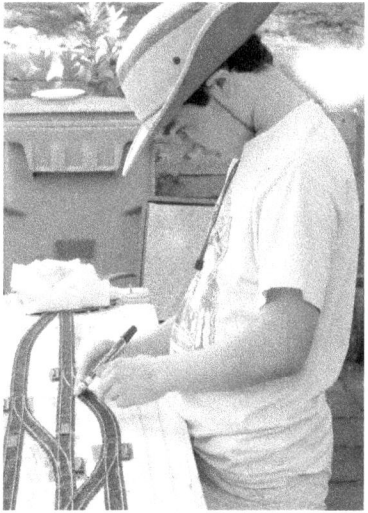

The Timesaver track

TRAIN SWITCHING YARD

Russell is a medium-high verbal autistic who loves trains and playing the guitar. His first project with us was a small HO scale switchyard based on John Allen's Timesaver. (HO is 1:87 scale and is the most popular scale for model railroads.) John Allen was a very creative American model railroader active from the 1940s to the 1970s. The Timesaver was a standardized design for a train switching puzzle that allows for interesting operating challenges in a very small space. This was a perfect project for Russell as it was firmly within his major area of interest: trains. He learned many new skills: how to solder, lay scale model track, create landscape scenery, and connect electrical wiring. When the Timesaver Track was finished, Russell spent many hours shuttling cars back and forth.

Sharing a joint focus is less anxiety producing.

When working on the Timesaver Track, Russell would often become very anxious and then enraged. Autistry staff created a behavioral plan with Russell that included doing push-ups whenever he became seriously anxious and angry. This had worked so successfully with Jeffrey that we hoped it would work for Russell too. It did. Pushups seem to be a great way to release pent up energy. They are also easy to do almost anywhere. They have become a useful tool in our self-regulation toolbox. The pushups are not punitive; they are more curative. And to reinforce this the mentors do pushups along with the students. Whoever suggests pushups for a student does the pushups themselves right alongside the student. We all become stronger.

HARVEY MILK AS ROLE MODEL

Corey was in high school when he joined one of our first workshops in the barn. He was acting out in destructive ways at school (stealing, skipping school), and he had nearly exhausted the possible school placements available. He came to our program not because he is autistic but because no other program seemed to help him.

We are your children

Corey was mostly charming to work with but would seemingly randomly screw up. It was a challenge for us to decipher what issues were creating the personal obstacles that he continually threw into his own path. We decided not to dig into the issues but to work with Corey in the present—on a project of his choosing.

He has always been an avid film buff, though he is less interested in the narrative of the film than he is in the metadata: the box office statistics, names of cast and crew, and other facts. For his first project, he chose to recreate a diorama of a scene from the film, *Milk*, the biography of Harvey Milk. Corey had recently come out as gay, so the theme of the film resonated with him. We all watched the film several times to find a scene that would work as a stand-alone diorama. Corey chose to create the scene where Harvey is sitting on the roof of a car in a parade down Castro Street in San Francisco. It was a great choice as the crowds with protest signs contributed to an informative and dynamic tableau.

The construction of the project itself was a challenge. Corey's sight is impaired. Though he can see, he is legally blind and had several eye

surgeries as an infant to correct the alignment of his eyes. It was a significant challenge for him to paint and assemble the miniatures needed for the diorama. However, he was so interested in the project that he stuck with it. Corey researched 1970s era San Francisco to find examples of signs and clothing. We ordered dozens of human figures that he carefully painted and positioned for the crowd scenes. Despite his sight issues, we held him to a high standard of production. It took several attempts, but he created a wonderfully detailed diorama.

Over the several months of working on the Harvey Milk project with his Autistry mentor, Corey had the opportunity to talk about his sexuality and what it was like for him to be gay in a straight world. This allowed him to work through much of his anxiety. By focusing on the creation of his project rather than the maladaptive behaviors that had caused so much trouble in school, Corey was able to stay engaged with the Autistry group and attend workshops regularly. He is still, more than ten years later, extremely proud of the Harvey Milk project.

Elf World – A special place

CREATIVE PROBLEM-SOLVING

William is a high verbal man in his late 30s. He is an experienced painter and paints many familiar still lifes and fantasy subjects. One day we were all making figures out of polymer clay. Polymer clays (common brand names are Sculpey and Fimo) are plastic clays available in many colors that can be hardened in a few minutes at very low temperatures (275° F/135° C). William swiftly made a charming little seated elf character with glasses. We were all very impressed with this figure, and we encouraged William to make a diorama of the elf's house in the forest. Many of the larger parts of the house were made with polymer clay, and they were too big to fit in our oven.

This was not going to stop production. In the spirit of "Where there's a will, there's a way," we hastily built an insulated enclosure of discarded large Styrofoam packing pieces. We hung powerful light bulbs inside and literally created our own Easy-Bake Oven. The oven worked that one time we needed it, but the Styrofoam melted too much to use it again.

William spent hours painting and detailing the elf's house. Creative problem-solving, perseverance, and attention to detail helped William create a very special world for his woodland creatures.

PROJECT CROSS POLLINATION

One of the unexpected benefits of doing individual projects in groups is that the students get inspired by the work of their peers. They look

at the workbench beside them and see something being built that they would not have thought of. One year we had a surge of remote-controlled car projects. The cars were not only educational and fun to make, running them elicited spontaneous social interaction. Groups of students would hold races in the hallway and out in the parking lot. We

Dirty cars after muddy driving

once took everyone to a dirt lot for an off-road driving adventure. It had rained the night before, so we returned to the studio wet, muddy, and laughing. An important lesson: in life you sometimes get dirty!

Another benefit of creating projects is experiencing the growth and maturation of our students as they learn new skills. Many will often create the same subject matter but in a more sophisticated way. Steven's line drawings of his character, Bupim, became 3D figures that became animated videos. When Ian was young,

The first project – Ian's foam hamburger

before we even started Autistry, he wanted to make a hamburger. We thought at first he was hungry, but   he said, "No, I want to make a toy hamburger."   Dan took him into the shop and they created a hamburger out of foam. Years later, working with an Autistry mentor, Ian again said he wanted to make a hamburger. But this time he wanted a large hamburger pillow. The mentor taught Ian how to sew and together they created a four-foot-high stuffed hamburger pillow.

Core Value #5: Explore project ideas with no judgment while holding project production to a high standard

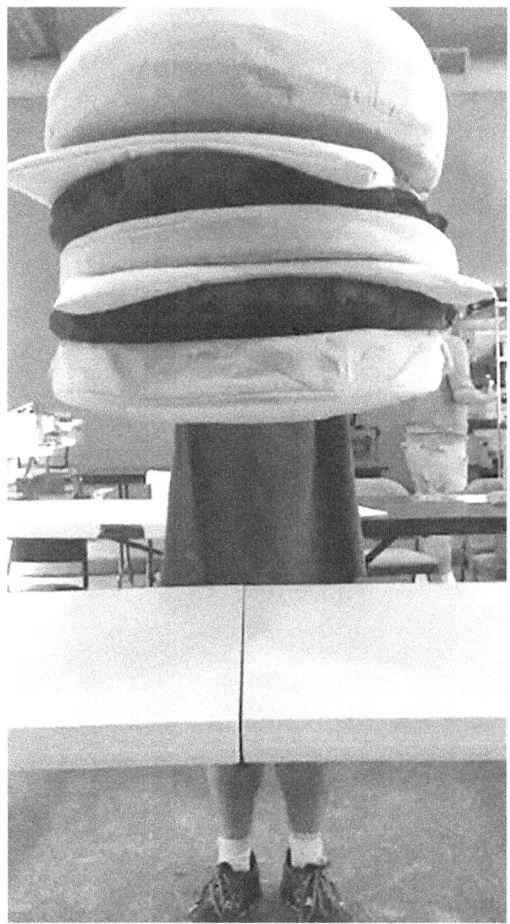

And then the burger pillow

CHAPTER 6

DOWNSIZING AND UPGRADING

The huge warehouse studio allowed the students to create large personal projects. We also took a few special orders. Our first commissioned piece was a 4 foot by 4 foot gar-

den shed. This order was very special as it came from Dr. Bryna Siegel, who, 15 years before, had diagnosed Ian with autism. At that time, Dr. Siegel had offered little hope for Ian's development, saying only that his sweet and engaging nature would endear him to his teachers. In that, she was not wrong. Delivering the

Ian delivers the garden shed to Dr. Bryna Siegel

garden shed that Ian and another Autistry student had built was a clear message that growth, development, and productivity are possible even for those young children for whom there seems little hope.

With the larger space we were also able to have larger equipment. With a grant from a local organization, we purchased a full-sized Shop-Bot. The ShopBot is a gantry tool, having a bridge from which a router (a power cutting tool) is suspended. The action of the router is controlled by software often referred to as CNC—Computerized Numerical Control. The ShopBot has become one of our most used and most loved tools. Because the router is driven by software, the students can input their designs and stay at a safe distance from the actual cutting. The ShopBot had an enormous impact on one of our students.

MACHINE BFF

When the ShopBot arrived, Lisa had been with us for just over a year.

She had originally failed our intake process as she did not have an autism diagnosis; in the in-person interview she was far more interested in the Autistry staff mentor than she was in any of the projects or tools. But the family was persistent, so we invited Lisa to attend a four-week summer camp. Lisa displayed considerable initial rigidity that we countered quite firmly with new (to her) boundaries. Our goals were to see if she could change, learn different responses, and avoid frustration meltdowns. Happily, Lisa displayed very rapid adaptation to the new boundaries. Her rate of learning was very high, which was inconsistent with the reports we had from her school program. We also noted Lisa successfully manipulating the staff to get what she wanted—a clear sign of intelligence.

Lisa showed very poor social empathy. When asked about others, Lisa became uncharacteristically grumpy, which with autistics typically means stress/fear. Lisa's social world can be modeled as the traditional

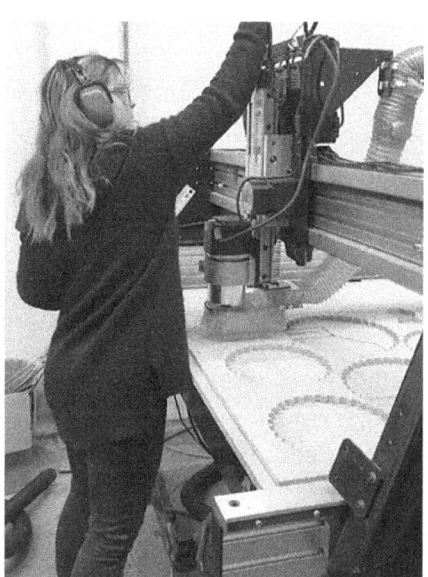

The ShopBot – everyone's favorite tool

autistic bubble-world. And it is a very small bubble. At the studio, Dan and a young mentor were allowed inside Lisa's bubble. In fact, they were the only people at the studio she could name—all others were simply "That person."

Though confused by human emotions, Lisa happily engaged empathically with machines: "He [the printer] is happy." "ShopBot does not like making that." Lisa was more comfortable imagining what machines think and feel than understanding what her human peers actually feel. The ShopBot quickly became her best friend. Working with Dan, Lisa helped assemble the ShopBot when it arrived. She learned how to set it up, run it, and maintain it. She also taught other students how to run the ShopBot and created a special role for herself at Autistry as the ShopBot instructor.

BIG SPACE, BIG PROBLEMS

For five years we enjoyed the large open space. We built dog houses, garden sheds, and even started (but didn't finish) a teardrop trailer. We worked on our remote- controlled cars in the middle of the shop floor and created a 12-foot racetrack out of cardboard for a fundraiser. The vast open area allowed us to literally Think Big. But there were downsides. The 10,000 square foot space, with its cement floor, tin roof, and no insulation, was impossible to heat in the winter and to air condition in the summer. When it rained, the tin roof echoed each raindrop, and the resulting cacophony made conversations difficult. The students came anyway.

As the popularity of the program grew, we were faced with increasing financial considerations. The rent for the warehouse was expensive, and more students meant hiring more staff. The workshops are private pay group therapy

10,000 square feet fills up fast

sessions, and we did not (and still don't) accept insurance. We explored other possible funding sources, including the Department of Rehabilitation (DOR) and the Department of Developmental Services (DDS).

The representative from the DOR rejected our request for support for several reasons, the first being there was no sidewalk leading from the main street to our warehouse at the end of the dead-end alley. That was an issue we had no control over. They then pointed out several other deal-breaking issues: open access to power tools, no wheelchair access to bathroom facilities, no accommodation for sight impaired individuals, limited heat and air conditioning control, and far too many sharp tools lying on work benches. Those issues we could have resolved with significant financial support that the DOR did not offer. So that funding avenue was not a viable option.

We explored other possible funding sources.

So we approached another source of public funding. In California, the DDS is responsible for coordinating the services and the funding for individuals with developmental disabilities—including autistics. The department handles this enormous task through a network of 21 non-profit agencies spread throughout the state. These agencies, called regional centers, do not provide direct services. The regional centers assess an individual's needs and eligibility for services and vendorize local agencies to provide those services. We applied to be a service providing agency.

PROTECTING OUR POWER TOOLS

The response from the representatives of our local regional center, the Golden Gate Regional Center (GGRC), was decidedly mixed. They were intrigued and impressed with our program. They were also adamant that they could not support a program with "dangerous" power tools. This was a dilemma for us: get funded or keep our power tools. There really was no choice. Autistics with Power Tools is one of our mottos and a fundamental part of our programs. We kept the power tools.

The chop-saw – one of the safest power tools in the shop

Why power tools? There are as many reasons to have power tools in the workshop as there are types of tools. A power drill provides the opportunity to practice focus, balance, eye-hand coordination, and adjusting one's position to create the drilling angle needed. A chop saw teaches alignment and develops measuring skills. The bandsaw seems particularly risky as the blade is exposed and moves quickly. But with proper instruction and oversight, the bandsaw is a great way to learn nuanced movement—careful shifting of a piece of wood to get the profile cut desired. The nail gun sounds like a deadly weapon but in fact is a fairly safe tool. It only "fires" when pressed against something, so it isn't possible to shoot someone from across the room. Any tool can be

Power tools are empowering.

dangerous if used carelessly, but the presence of risk helps to sharpen the senses.

In 2015, our five-year lease on the warehouse was up for renewal. Ownership of the warehouse had changed several times over that period. The new owners raised our rent to more realistically reflect the market value. It had been a challenge to meet all our expenses at the original below market level. We had become quite creative in our fundraising events: the Cardboard Carnival, the Scientists & Artists Party, the Handmade Model RC Car Race, and many other fabulous activities. We managed to keep the organization afloat with fees and fundraising— but only barely.

We put the word out on the autism grapevine that we were searching for a new studio. We looked at several places, but none had what we needed—a combination of workshop space and comfortable space. We needed a hybrid of the warehouse and our home. Most of the facilities we saw were rather cold and industrial.

DOWNSIZING

Our realtor found an unusual property on DuBois Street only a few blocks from our warehouse. We worried at first that we would be going from 10,000 square feet down to 5,000 square feet, but when we walked in the door, we knew he was right. This new warehouse was a combination of homey and industrial—just the kind of odd space we needed. The offices were finished with wood trim and the hallway floor was flagstone. The large meeting room had a stage and skylights with controllable shades. We were surprised to find refrigerated drawers in several built-in cabinets—and a freezer drawer that would quickly become the Popsicle Station. But the best feature was the heat and air-conditioning. The actual shop area was smaller than we would have liked, but the overall feel of the space and the several discrete areas easily made up for the smaller shop.

By the time we moved into the Du Bois Street studio, we had been running Project-Based Therapy Workshops for seven years. Our initial workshop group of four students had grown to five workshops with four to six students each. We created cohorts based on age and verbal ability. When Asperger's Syndrome was dropped from the DSM-V in 2013, the term High-Functioning Autism began to be used more frequently to describe autistics with unimpaired language and normal to high intelligence. But high-functioning/low-functioning are such vague and rather demeaning terms that we tend to categorize (when we need to) our students as High-Verbal and Low-Verbal. This

High-functioning is a vague and rather demeaning term.

simply gives us an idea of their ability to communicate verbally but does not prejudge the content or sophistication of what they would like to communicate.

The five workshops, which came to be called Core Workshops, run from Thursday through Sunday. We have a group of older adults

(30s-early 50s) on Thursday afternoons, our transition age (18-20s) on Fridays, and teenagers (13-18) on the weekends. These are all private pay Project-Based Therapy groups. The Project-Based Therapy workshops are expensive because they are resource intensive. We staff nearly 1:1 to give

It's all about the relationships

maximum support and to build strong trusting relationships. As each student creates their own project, there is a large need for a wide variety of materials, tools, and equipment.

We had not set out to create programs solely for wealthy autistics, but it was becoming impossible for us to personally cover the budget shortfalls. We were in the impossible situation that with every new student we added, we lost more money. Fundraising was also becoming difficult. When our son was a young boy, we had raised money for the

We are adults so much longer than we are children.

public school system to support the education of special needs children. Janet was active in Dedication to Special Education (DSE), an organization of parents who realized that their children with learning challenges were expensive to educate and easy for the school system to ignore. DSE has raised millions of dollars in the last 20 years and brought our children out of the

hidden special classrooms and into the light. Photographs of six year old boys and girls with wide eyes and wider smiles had donors immediately reaching for their checkbooks. Photos of adults with challenges do not solicit the same response. This surprised us since the needs of adults are so much greater; we are adults so much longer than we are children. It should be a natural part of the life-cycle: when children become adults, the parents step back. But autistic children, and those with other challenges, continue to need support, often throughout their lifetime.

STICKING TO OUR (NAIL) GUNS

Very proud puppeteers

We were determined, despite the financial challenges, to continue the workshops. Put simply, they worked. The students gained both soft social skills and hard vocational skills. They enjoyed the workshops and took great pride in creating unique projects of their own design. Given the opportunity to explore their interests, they not only created cool projects but learned about themselves. With the help of the mentors, the students began to discover what obstacles were getting in the way of their success. They became more confident, less passive, and better able to take the risks that would lead to growth. We knew if we compromised on the power tools and stopped challenging our students, we would be recreating yet another recreational macaroni art program.

The families also saw the benefit of the workshops. They reported positive changes in their autistic sons and daughters: better self-regulation, more language, and less depression. The most common remark was that their child had found direction. This did not happen immediately, of course, but very gradually over time.

Still, we had to find a way to support our students over the long run in order to see progress. The families began to push on the GGRC, asking why it was not funding the Autistry program. Most of the students were already clients of GGRC, or they qualified for services but had not yet applied. We received a call from GGRC one day, asking about our new space and how that might affect our ability to be funded. Before they would consider funding us they required that we obtain a Community Care License (CCL). Having a CCL effectively spreads the liability and oversight issues over several organizations (DDS, GGRC, and Autistry). It was a reasonable request, but we feared, given our earlier experience with the Department of Rehabilitation, that we would not be able to qualify for that license.

SOMETIMES LIFE SMILES

The inspector sent by CCL was an avid maker. He loved the workshop, especially the power tools and the ShopBot. He totally understood our process and our maker-spirit philosophy. He saw the value of hands-on creation because he had experienced it himself. There were many aspects of the studio that needed to be upgraded and several changes to be made, like locks on all the doors leading to the shop area. But we could keep our power tools and our other equipment. And, if we made the changes to the environment, we would get a Community Care License. We made the changes.

With our license in hand, we set up a meeting with GGRC. That meeting led to the creation of a program we had never before envisioned: the Autistry Comprehensive Adult Program (ACAP). This is basically a day program but one unlike any we had seen before.

Team power drilling

***Core Value #6: Stay focused on what works,
not what gets funded***

CHAPTER 7

DAY PROGRAM

After several tours of post-high school programs, we vowed never to run a day program. Adult day programs generally provide recreational and social activities for individuals with non-medical issues. They rarely provide educational or vocational activities. The term itself conjures up visions of zombies playing card games or day care centers where parents drop off children and go to work. What we wanted for our adult son and for others facing social and vocational challenges was not day-long babysitting but a program that encouraged growth and led to the highest level of independence possible.

NEVER SAY NEVER

Yet as we explored our funding options with the GGRC, we soon realized that the best option for us was, in fact, the day program model. It allowed us to offer a full day of workshops five days a week. It also kept the groups together; many other funding options, such as Tailored Day Services, are based on programs for individuals. Tailored Day Services is a great program for providing very individualized support. Unfortunately, as it stands now, an individual cannot have Tailored Day with any other concurrent day service. It was important to us as we wrestled with the design of a day program not to lose what we had learned after years of

Small group on a long hike

offering group workshops. The workshop groups of five or six students fostered social interaction and helped to create a community. But those

groups only met once a week for four hours. We were now looking at how to fill 30 hours a week (five six-hour days).

We approached this problem by taking a deep look at our overarching goal: to build independent adults. What does independence mean? We arrived at this definition: *Independence is the ability to plan and make progress towards desired long-term goals while adequately handling imme-*

Self-portrait with pride

diate needs as they arise.

That's a mouthful, but what we identified was the need to have a target (the long-term goal) that sets you on a path forward and the individual self-control/self-regulation to solve the problems that would inevitably block your path. We see independence as part of forward motion, part of growing. Once you stop moving forward, you become dependent on others for food and shelter—on family, or public programs, or past achievement (savings). If you stop taking the initiative, you also become dependent on others for social activities and recreation. You become a passive participant in your own life.

SECRET SAUCE RECIPE

We identified several key ingredients in the recipe for independence, which are the abilities to:
- to challenge yourself
- to educate yourself
- to take care of yourself
- to control (regulate) yourself
- to find sustainable engagement with your community (vocation or volunteer)

Independence is not about going it alone. Independence is about going forward in the direction of your choice and that often means asking for help.

First, **independence requires the ability to challenge yourself.**

With over a decade of experience working with neurodivergent teens and adults, we know that our students grow and develop when appropriately challenged. We also know that left unchallenged, they will regress. We receive dozens of phone calls every week from parents reporting that their transition-age or adult child does not want to leave their room where they are glued to the computer screen.

Jerry's father called us one day with a very familiar story: "My 23-year-old son has no friends, watches tv or plays video games all day, and does not participate in family activities." Jerry came in for an interview. He was rather shy but articulate and quite knowledgeable about particular television shows—the few he did watch, he watched without fail. **It was a slow process**
He especially liked long-running series. He could retell the plots of all the episodes of *Dr. Who*, and he knew which episode of *Supernatural* appeared in which season. Jerry saw himself as a creative artist. Using an online program, he designed computer-generated characters. The program provided the characters and gave the user several options for customizing them. He was actually choosing elements rather than creating—much like customizing a car.

We worked with Jerry to explore his early childhood interests as a gateway to learning new skills and igniting motivation. We have boxes of LEGOS, and he began to create new characters with them—a more hands-on version of the online programs. We challenged Jerry to use LEGO play to inspire his own characters. It was a slow process, but as Jerry discovered his unique vision, he became more confident and more engaged with others. Though never comfortable in large group settings, Jerry did develop appropriate social skills and began to interact with his peers at Autistry.

With this new confidence and social ability Jerry was able to move out of the family home into a supported living situation with his peers. He now works part-time at a local grocery store.

Chris joined Autistry when he was 14 years old and in middle school. He had poor social and executive functioning skills and a profound speech impairment. He had been placed in a non-public school because of his need for significant individual support. The placement worked well for him for the first year, but then the school began to

Working together on the helmet

take on more students with serious behavioral issues, and the environment changed. Chris was now surrounded by peers who were screaming, throwing things, and eventually being restrained by the staff. This caused him great anxiety and self-doubt and led to regression rather than progress.

In the Core Workshop, Chris worked closely with a mentor on several creative and complex projects. His intelligence and curiosity were apparent from day one. He quickly chose to make a Star Wars helmet. Over the course of several months, the helmet took shape and Chris gained confidence. It was a process of continued challenge—overcoming construction mistakes and having to start again, overcoming fine-motor issues in order to produce the helmet he envisioned, and working to communicate effectively with his mentor to get the help he needed.

With this new confidence Chris was ready to take the huge step of returning to public school. He began gradually by taking one and then two classes at his local high school while still attending the non-public school. Chris adapted quickly and soon was taking a full academic load at high school. He graduated with honors and, with support from Autistry, he enrolled in the community college. At this writing, Chris is just two classes away from completing an AA degree.

The work with Jerry, Chris, and others showed us that when challenged and given the appropriate support, individuals will thrive. But

left unchallenged, individuals regress. They can become totally dependent on their families for sustenance and often dependent on the video gaming industry for entertainment.

Second, **independence requires the ability to take care of yourself.**

The Washington State Department of Social and Health Services developed The Independent Living Skills Assessment Tool to identify where an individual was along the path toward independent living. It is a checklist of skill levels in fifteen categories, including personal appearance and hygiene, health, food management, and emergency and safety skills. We updated the questions to reflect the advances in technology, and we rewrote some of them to make them more applicable and more accessible to our students. For example, we added "knows how to use a debit card" and "knows how to use a CalFresh card" (the food stamp program card in California). These questions are more in line with our students' experience than "knows how to write a check." But, in general, we found the Washington State assessment tool to be very informative. The questions are progressive, building in sophistication and skill level within each category.

Learning how to shop at the local grocery store

The categories are divided into four sections: Basic, Intermediate, Advanced, and Exceptional. For each section there is a required number of pieces of knowledge or skills needed before moving on to a more advanced section of questions. For example, in the category of Housekeeping, to move from Basic to Intermediate level the student must know three of the four skills:

1) Can wash dishes adequately using soap and hot water
2) Can change a light bulb
3) Can make a bed
4) Knows how to dispose of garbage

Most of our students will answer yes to each question

The information we gain from this assessment can be very helpful if—and this is essential—the interviewer asks follow-up questions. Most of our students will answer yes to each question, but when asked to describe the activity step-by-step, they often struggle to provide details. Usually, the student understands the concept of washing dishes and has observed someone washing dishes but has little experience of actually doing it themselves. By equating passive observing with active experience, the student creates a false sense of their actual skill level. This can cause problems socially and in the workplace.

Aaron was very excited when hired by a local recycling center. He was absolutely capable of performing the job tasks, he arrived to work on time, and he was always dressed appropriately. However, he was not showering or washing his hair regularly or using deodorant. The job required a lot of physical activity in warm weather, and the situation soon became uncomfortable. As we had helped place Aaron in the job, his supervisor reached out to us for help.

"I take great care of my teeth. I just brushed them on Monday!"

When we discussed the situation with Aaron, his response was that he did shower regularly—at least twice a week. And he washed his clothes monthly. Once Aaron understood the need to shower daily and do his laundry at least weekly, he changed his routine and was able to keep his job.

From the early days of the Autistry program we encountered the need to remind or instruct individuals in matters of hygiene. One young man in our Thursday workshop replied to a mentor's inquiry on dental health with, "I take great care of my teeth. I just brushed them on Monday!" We found the most effective approach was the direct approach. Nuanced, generalized or cryptic remarks, like "Deodorant is helpful on warm days," were met with blank stares or non-committal head nods. But "Your body odor has reached a level where deodorant or a shower is absolutely necessary" kick-started a conversation about the individual's

hygiene routine and opened up a discussion on possible new strategies.

Third, **independence requires the ability to educate yourself.**

We are both firm believers in lifelong learning. Neither of us followed a traditional education path. We each have two master's degrees. Dan has an MS in Astronomy and another in Physics. Janet has an MS in Library and Information Science and another in Counseling Psychology. We easily have two decades of higher education between us. We value the learning process as much as the knowledge acquired. Education is not just going to school. Education opens the mind to new experiences of all kinds,

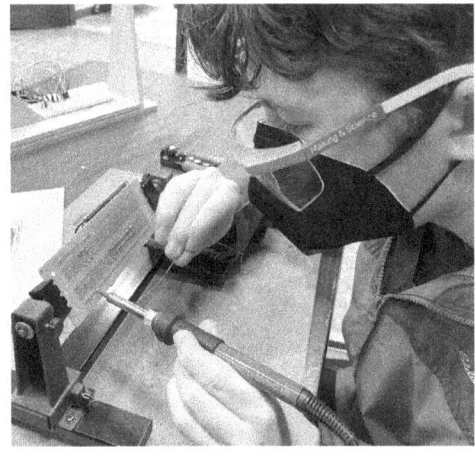

Soldering a very delicate circuit

large and small. This can be as simple as deciphering IKEA instructions or as complex as building a rocket.

Dan's educational history is not unlike the high school experience of many of our students. In high school Dan excelled in his vocational electronics class, was gifted in math, and read at an exceptional rate but got relentlessly poor grades in everything, totally baffling his teachers. He graduated from high school in 1979 when autism and learning differences were not understood or even acknowledged. Dan had been in programs for the gifted when he was younger. By high school he was seen as quiet and unremarkable. Dan was not encouraged to go to college despite his exceptionally good SAT scores because at the same time his GPA was basically a D. Dan applied at the last moment to Sonoma State University and thinks that the only reason he was accepted was that there were available seats for local high school students.

Dan majored in Physics and loved his classes but struggled immediately and was promptly placed on academic probation. After two years, he flunked out. After several tough years, Dan got back to college through a program offered by his employer and started taking night classes. He immediately got good grades and returned to school full time. And he immediately struggled again.

Dan found that taking a full class load, four or five classes, was very difficult, and he usually failed or did not complete two or three classes each semester. School counselors were confused. His being able to get A's and B's in virtually any class, as long as he only took one or two classes, was confusing to them. "Surely, if you took more classes, you'd get C's at least?" Dan tried and just flunked everything. Dan learned that he needed to take a small class load but did not understand why,. He continued in school this way all the way through a Ph.D. program in Astrophysics.

> **Quality and persistence is more important than quantity and speed**

All of this is a long way of saying that we understand our students need different paths to continue learning as adults and that quality and persistence is more important than quantity and speed.

OH, YES HE CAN

A high school special education teacher brought a young man to our program. She described him as intelligent, creative, and fun to work with. But, she said, he cannot read. She gave no medical reason for

Autistry students take Biology 107!

this inability. He wasn't dyslexic. He was highly verbal with a fairly so-phisticated vocabulary. But she insisted that Carl could not read.

We accepted Carl into our program, and we soon realized that, in fact, he could read. He was quite capable of reading the instructions for video games that he wanted to play or to do online searches for information that he needed. He did not, however, read books or even long paragraphs. We approached this issue slowly as it was quite apparent that reading was an emotional subject for him. We began with graphic novels—lots of drawings and very little text.

Reading the graphic novels widened Carl's view of the world and gave him a more solid understanding of history.

As Carl's confidence grew, he began to overcome his fear of reading. He chose books from our library about films that he loved and read them independently. He also began to share with us his more complex creative ideas for short stories and videos. Carl may never be an avid reader, but with a group of other Autistry students he took and passed an English class at the local community college. He proved the special education teacher wrong—he could learn to read, and he could succeed academically. This ability to read has allowed Carl to learn more about the topics he loves—animals, art, and design. But most importantly, Carl has a desire to educate himself.

We work closely with College of Marin, our local community college. Our son Ian took every remedial math course offered there and finally passed the math class needed for his AA requirement. He has yet to finish the other courses necessary for the degree, but he, like our other Autistry students, is comfortable navigating the college campus and taking college classes.

We hope that all our students develop a love of learning as that is part of the recipe for independence.

Fourth, **independence requires the ability to control yourself.**

When looking at the way forward for our students, we try to identify the obstacles in their path, obstacles that they have some control over. One area that is difficult to address but has a huge impact on their ability to engage in community activities is personal behavior. Behaviors that are destructive to the individual's ability to participate in the community need to be identified and managed. Most autistics, as well as most neurotypicals, have routines for self-soothing. In the autism world we call this stimming—self-stimulating behavior that is often repetitive movements, sounds, or phrases.

> Most autistics, as well as most neurotypicals, have routines for self-soothing

Ian likes to throw a ball from one hand to another or bounce up and down. He has developed very large calf muscles from "toe-walking"— striding without dropping his heels down. Some of our other students have more common stimming behaviors like hand-flapping or rocking back and forth or verbal stims like repeating phrases or certain noises. These are not aggressive or even inappropriate behaviors when done in an appropriate environment. They are, however, distracting or disturbing behaviors when done in a crowded public space and can create a barrier to community engagement.

Research scientists are only just beginning to understand the interplay between emotions and our body chemicals. We know that emotions are basically complex chemical reactions, signals sent through our bodies via neurotransmitters leading to a behavioral response. Stimming is a behavioral response, and though stimming is a common method of self-soothing for neuro-typical as well as neurodi-vergent individuals (who hasn't tapped their fingers on the desk when concentrating or hummed a tune to calm down?), many autistics have a heightened or more intense sensory experience of the world—they feel things strongly. Their response to stimuli (oral, physical, or visual) can also be stronger, so their stims can be larger and last longer. We now know that the

Sometimes you just gotta jump

Marine drill sergeant reprimanded Dan for stimming and that Dan's behavior was an example of his autistic nature.

Finding effective calming strategies is important to maintain positive social engagement.

Fifth, **independence requires the ability to sustain engagement with your community.**

What we learned from our employment experiences is that getting a job is one thing, keeping it is quite another.

Perhaps the greatest obstacle to an independent life is the difficulty of finding sustainable employment, either paid or volunteer.

Many hands make light work

Realistically, the job market is tough; highly educated neurotypical individuals now compete with less educated or less experienced individuals for entry level positions. Most of our students receive support funding from the Department of Disability Services, so they generally do not need high paying jobs. However, employment is one of the main ways we interact with our community and how we define ourselves.

There are several local, state, and even national programs that offer to find jobs for autistics, claiming their special skills can be a valuable asset to a company. But successful employment is more than just possessing a set of skills; it is the ability to work with others, work for others, and work in spite of others. If a large paycheck is not a necessity, volunteering at an organization of high interest is a feasible alternative to a paying but less engaging job.

> **Successful employment is more than just possessing a set of skills**

Julie is a highly intelligent and well educated young woman. She has applied for, been hired, and subsequently fired from many jobs. It was difficult to figure out from the termination letters what was causing the employment failures. The letters most always praised Julie's job performance but then stated that she was not a good fit for their business environment. When we discussed this with Julie and asked her to tell us in detail about her day, we realized that it was the social aspects of the job that were difficult for her. She reported feeling uncomfortable in the cafeteria surrounded by co-workers who all seemed to know each other and were engaged in lively conversations. She, on the other hand, sat alone and grew more and more anxious. As she described the experience, she became agitated and began to mumble under her breath. "The sound of all those voices hurt my ears." she said. "I tried to cover my ears, but that didn't work. I finally brought headphones so that I could block out the noise."

We knew from working with Julie that, when anxious, her mumbling could become full-throated vocalizing. We could imagine what her co-workers would have seen: a young woman, sitting alone, ears covered with headphones, talking loudly to herself. Most people who have no experience with autistics will often confuse self-regulating behavior (stimming)—especially loud self-talk—with "crazy behavior." Many neurotypicals become very uncomfortable with this behavior and view it as "not a good fit for their business environment."

Autistics have a reputation for stubbornness

Stimming is not the only obstacle to successful employment. Other behaviors, habits, and social interchanges can cause misunderstanding and friction in the workplace. Autistics have a reputation for stubbornness, an unwillingness to let go of an opinion or viewpoint, making negotiation a nonstarter. This is referred to as cognitive rigidity and is defined as an inability to adapt to changes in information or to accept information that contradicts previously held beliefs. This is also often referred to as rigid thinking. In the workplace this resistance to change can cause an autistic employee to push back on tasks they feel are not right for some reason.

Dana works at a garden center. She loves plants and is friendly and helpful with the customers. She also has a passion for weeding. Any perceived weed on the property or popping up in a plant display was in peril of being plucked out by Dana. This would not have been a serious problem if Dana's knowledge of plants had been sufficient to distinguish between weed and nascent flower. But while her knowledge was weak, her passion was strong. This gave rise to several confrontations with the store management. Dana dug in her heels, claiming that she was doing great work at keeping pesky weeds away. We worked closely with the management, and after several instances of "random" weeding—and many discussions—Dana finally agreed to only pull out plants that had been identified by her supervisor as weeds. Dana nearly lost her job over this rigidity, and she still battles her inner weed demons, but by putting in place a system of check-ins, she was able to overcome the knee-jerk urge to weed. We are now working on the fine points of deadheading!

Having identified the five key ingredients in the recipe for independence, we were ready to design a day program: the Autistry

Comprehensive Adult Program (ACAP). After nearly a decade of providing private-pay therapeutic build stuff workshops, we were ready to tackle the challenge of creating a program funded by the GGRC and overseen by the DSS. How to create a program that would develop and support the fundamental ingredients for independence, meet the requirements of these two agencies, and stay true to our core values became our personal challenge.

All in this together

When we finally submitted the design for the five-day Autistry Comprehensive Adult Program (ACAP), the curriculum contained four interwoven programs: Education, Life Skills, Physical Fitness/Healthy Living, and Vocation. Together these programs provide a learning experience that supports growth, maturation, and individuation.

Our first semester we had 12 students. As of this writing we have 27 enrolled in the ACAP program. Each student has unique goals. but there are common areas of need that allow us to create small cohorts. At the beginning of each semester, we look at each student's progress and then choose cohorts who are at similar points in their arc of growth. One cohort has a goal of attaining an AA Degree from community college and then transferring to a four-year college. Another group needs remedial courses in English and Math to gain academic skills they had either lost or never acquired. Some students are more interested in training for employment and need to acquire social and vocational skills. Those who only want a recreational program are referred to other organizations. For us, recreation is a reward for hard work, not a way of life.

Core Value #7: Respect and support the many aspects of independence

CHAPTER 8

EDUCATION

To support continued education and lifelong learning, the Autistry Comprehensive Adult Program (ACAP) provides in-class mentors, homework assistance, college registration help, and coursework organization. Most of our students take at least one community college course per semester. We also lead reading and writing groups at the studio for students who are not ready yet or are not interested in taking college courses but who want to continue to expand their knowledge.

Studying at the local library

We encourage students to take only one class their first college semester. As Dan learned from his academic experience, several classes mean several transitions, and transitions are difficult. Transitions take time and energy away from study and cause anxiety. Most of our Autistry students were either in special education classes or heavily supported in mainstream classes during their elementary and high school years. Learning how to navigate the campus, finding the classrooms, and preparing for the classes is enough of a challenge without adding multiple courses.

Students who apply for financial support or on-campus housing often face a dilemma: to qualify for support, a student must be full-time, taking 12 or more units, which is usually three or four classes. For neurodivergent individuals this can be a setup for failure. When asked by policymakers and politicians what we would change to help our students, the full-time student requirement is top of our list. For many students, taking two classes is full time.

LEARNING DIFFERENTLY

Many of our students need support in the classroom since the material is often presented in a way that is difficult for them to follow, especially in the heavily verbal lecture classes. We work closely with the college accessibility departments and arrange to send our staff into the classroom with the students. The Autistry in-class college mentors function much like translators, rendering academic lectures into the

> **Some students process information visually—they literally see what you're saying**

unique language of each student. Some students process information visually—they literally see what you're saying. For these

Rocket science on the whiteboard

students, creating visual aids is essential. Over the years the Autistry mentors have made models of the circulatory system for students taking human biology, created board games to help students understand and remember terms in English class, built complex dioramas to bring to life historical events, and come up with many other intriguing visual translations.

Another aspect of visual learning that is common amongst autistics is the visualization of information. Temple Grandin, in her 2022 book, *Visual Thinking: The Hidden Gifts of People Who Think in Pictures, Patterns, Abstractions*, describes visual thinkers as seeing "images in their mind's eye that allow them to make rapid-fire associations." Dr. Grandin also points out that "we live in a talky culture." That verbal-based culture often devalues the imagistic associations made by visual thinkers.

Dan's visual thinking was highlighted in his first Ph.D. level astrophysics class at Indiana University. The professor wrote a problem on the board, confident no student would solve it. The other students scribbled pages of equations. Dan raised his hand and said "L." Although he was the only student to give the correct answer, he received only partial credit because he did not have the equations to support it. He pictured the mathematical process in his mind and arrived at the solution. His "rapid-fire association" was acknowledged but not celebrated as a unique and potentially powerful ability.

Other students are auditory learners. They process, understand, and remember what they have heard rather than what they have read. For these students it is often helpful to read assignments aloud to them. We also found that reading test questions aloud to auditory learners improves their exam performance by increasing their understanding and decreasing their anxiety. Test-taking accommodations are part of a student's accessibility agreement with the school and usually need to have been put in place before the class starts. Other accommodations could include priority seating, recording devices, note-taking help, and extended time for tests and in-class assignments.

Hands-on learning

An often overlooked processing style is kinetic or hands-on learning. Kinetic learners learn by doing. This is where Project-Based teaching is most impactful. Sewing, cooking, and model-building all offer tangible learning opportunities—especially for math skills. Math can be

Kinetic learners learn by doing.

a very abstract concept but also can be a very down-to-earth process for figuring out the correct payload for a backyard rocket or the perfect size base for a Lord of the Rings diorama. When used to measure the correct amount of brown sugar to add to chocolate chip cookie dough, math becomes an essential means to a very yummy end.

Kinetic learners also process information best when moving around. Sitting in long lecture classes can be difficult and almost painful for them. We have negotiated classroom accommodations for students to be allowed to quietly leave class, walk up and down the hallway, and then return to their seat whenever they need to physically regulate their thoughts. Chewing gum can also be helpful but may need special accommodations from the professor.

Built into the ACAP schedule is supported homework and class debriefing time. The mentors and students return to the studio or work on campus to review the class material and decode the professor's lecture. The students have often missed important details of the verbal lectures because many of our students process auditory information more slowly than professors speak. The mentors take notes during class to catch the essential details. Learning takes time and effort.

COLLEGE COURSES

Just as we challenge our students to rise above the low expectation of Macaroni Art, we challenge our students to take mainstream college classes. We recognize that many students need to begin by taking remedial courses to improve their math, reading, and general study abilities. We encourage them to enroll in an academic course as soon as they are ready. We are continually amazed at how well our students do in academic courses when given the proper support.

Not all professors welcome our diverse learners into their classrooms. We have encountered strong elitist and prejudicial attitudes from professors who assume students who lack verbal fluency also lack intelligence. Most professors are surprised and positively amazed to discover the insight and comprehension that is masked by communication difficulties. Others, sadly, refuse to accept the possibility that verbal ability is not the only indication of

Study materials

intelligence. We keep a list of professors who "get it" and a list of those who don't.

Studying all together

We advise our students to avoid those professors who will make their academic journey more difficult since the task ahead of them is difficult enough. But if, due to lack of alternative offerings, they must take a class from a narrow-minded professor, we support the students advocating for themselves using all the avenues available, including lodging a formal complaint of discrimination if that is called for.

Multimedia courses are very popular with our students since so many are quite adept at playing online games. The students quickly learn that playing a video game and writing code for a video game are two quite different activities. Their strong attraction to the subject matter provides leverage for us to challenge them to learn software programming and sophisticated software programs.

We now have several students who are on track to receive a certificate or an Associate of Arts degree in Multimedia Studies. It is an intensive program that includes graphic design and web design as well as game development. As always, we start each student in one class at a time so that they can develop the skills as well as the necessary study habits to be successful. We schedule several hours of homework help during the week. For one three-hour-a-week class we provide as many as three two-hour study sessions—basically twice the time of the actual class. This is another example of how learning takes time—and even more time for the neurodivergent.

We start each student in one class at a time

Students aiming for an AA degree are required to take several general education courses in English, science, humanities, and the arts. These courses can be a real challenge since they often do not align directly with our students' interests. It is a challenge for our mentors to help our students find a connection to the material. Before registering for classes, we talk with each student to identify a compelling interest, including but not limited to historic issues, current politics, rock formations, animals, etc. As our funding is based on a 2:1 staffing, we create cohorts of at least two students for each course. We are also careful not to send all of our 27 students into the same class; that could overwhelm the professor and also would defeat the purpose of an integrated education.

Alex is a highly anxious young man with a deep interest in politics and social issues. He tends to perseverate on negative social trends and can become quite agitated when discussing what he perceives as a "path toward the end of society." Alex was both extremely attracted to and very dysregulated by political conversations. He would become visibly upset and take on a rigid position from which he would lecture those around him about how people should think and how things should be.

We were hesitant to suggest a humanities course since the material might trigger even more anxiety. Because he was pursuing an AA degree and because of his interest in politics and history, we went forward with first an anthropology course and then a history course that discusses elements such as racism, fascism, and sexism. By looking at politics and history as intense special interests, we were able to follow the earlier lessons we learned from our Project-Based Therapy work: by joining with the student in their interest and moving towards it instead of away from it, we are able to build flexibility and collaboration, turning monologues into dialogues. The rigid interest often softens and loses its obsessional quality when the student explores the interest more deeply and shares with a mentor.

Because we engaged with Alex in the exploration of his interest through structured college courses, he has made continued growth in his ability to discuss challenging current and historical events. In his current class, he is often a leader in class discussions and expresses his strong opinions with skill while also listening to the input of others and maintaining a learning mindset. This growth has generalized outside of the classroom, and Alex now frequently engages in thoughtful and meaningful conversations with mentors and peers about subjects that we used to avoid.

We mentioned earlier that our son took a series of remedial math courses before passing the math requirement for an AA degree. He now is one class shy of the English requirement. Unfortunately, the remedial pathway that worked so well for him is no longer available. In 2017, California passed legislation (AB 705) with the goal of

Ian doing math homework

minimizing the length of time students remain in community college and maximizing the rate of transfer-level course completion within one year. The motivation for the legislation was noble—to prevent students being placed in remedial courses and thus extending their college years and potentially running out of funding before graduation. But the result at many colleges was that the remedial courses were eliminated and replaced with generic study skills classes.

This impacted our neurodiverse learners in several ways. The remedial or preparatory courses were no longer available, and there was now a push for students to fulfill math and English requirements within a year. Most of our students had not received fundamental math and English lessons in high school. They arrive at Autistry unprepared for college classes. The remedial pathway provided an opportunity for them to gain an education. The one-year goal for transfer course completion punishes students who process more slowly and learn on a different timeline. It is, quite simply, discriminatory.

> **It is, quite simply, discriminatory.**

AUTISTRY APPROACH TO EDUCATION

Our Autistry staff are very creative and invent fun and engaging methods of supporting our students. For those students with limited writing skills, we often use a graphic novel software program, Comic Life, which allows the students to create a narrative with images. The images can be uploaded easily into a storyboard grid, and dialogue bubbles can be added.

Learning can be fun

Raymond loves Disney characters. His first Comic Life project was simply uploading images of Simba, Nala, Ariel, Belle, and others into the grid and typing short bits of dialogue into the bubbles: "We need to hide from Scar" or "I'm looking for a prince."

When Raymond was comfortable with the software, we showed him how to upload his own photos and how to edit them. He could then add himself to the graphic narrative. He could interact with the characters. This simple process allowed Raymond to tell personal stories and write short essays. If, as Grant Morrison wrote, we live in the stories we tell ourselves, then helping students tell their story helps them discover themselves. Often those who have communication challenges are denied access to storytelling and struggle with identity. A simple image-based storyboard can open up a world of self-discovery.

> **We live in the stories we tell ourselves**

Pixar, the computer animation film studio based in the San Francisco Bay Area, now offers an online course in storytelling. Story Xperiential is a nine-week course with a well-developed curriculum that takes the student step by step through the process of creating a story. The goal of the class is for each student or team of students to create a story reel, a short image-based rendering of an animated narrative. The Pixar course is a more sophisticated version of our Comic Life projects with the added perk of hearing weekly presentations from professional writers and storyboard artists. It is a very well-constructed program, and we are incorporating it into our offerings. As with a college course, the Pixar program works best with support from mentors and designated time for homework.

ALL THE WORLD'S A STAGE

Another successful Autistry expansion is our Theater Arts Department.

Many of our students enjoy and benefit from drama courses at the community college. The voice and movement classes significantly improve their speech and increase their self-confidence. But the college is an academic institution and has certain rules and constraints, one of which is that students cannot take a class multiple times. Our students often need repetition in order to attain any degree of mastery. Though we continue to work closely with the community college drama department, we now offer drama classes at Autistry.

In 2021, Tim Flavin joined us as the Autistry Director of Theater Arts. Tim is a seasoned performer with more than 40 years of stage experience in the UK and the US. As the brother of an autistic, Tim also has a lifetime of experience with neurodiverse learners. That combination of professional and personal experience makes Tim a perfect fit for Autistry.

Drama group at the Belrose Theater

Without the time and curriculum constraints of the college system, Tim is able to create activities in response to the students' needs rather than adhere to a strict syllabus. He has developed a warm-up routine with the students that incorporates repetitive dance steps as well as several cross-lateral body movements, like crossing one leg over another to pivot in a new direction, touching the left elbow to the right knee, or doing high "Rockette kicks." These fundamental movements engage both sides of the body and encourage coordination. Both brain hemispheres are involved and activated, which leads to increased focus and cognitive functioning. We have found that the improved focus carries over into improved ability to concentrate on homework.

Mental focus and cognitive functioning are further enhanced by working with a script. Most autistics have difficulty dealing with abstraction. They will quickly lose interest in doing exercises and reading scripts with no end goal other than "It is good for you." Tim either writes or finds a short play that the students perform at the end of each semester. The performances are enlightening. Students who seem shy or disengaged often come alive in front of an audience.

Mike surprised us all. He is a quiet guy who generally keeps his head down and his shoulders pulled inward. Though he worked hard, he had difficulty memorizing his lines for the holiday play. His focus would wander during rehearsals. Mike had become reliant on the off-stage prompts from the stage manager and would break character to ask for lines. We were concerned that perhaps his working memory was not up to the task of holding all the dialogue in his head.

"It is good for you" will quickly lose their interest.

On the night of the performance, the house lights went down, the stage lights came up, and Mike calmed himself down and transformed into The Grinch. Gone was the hesitation, the distraction, and the searching for lines. Like a professional thespian, Mike absorbed the energy of the audience, using it to help him focus. When he stumbled on a line, he ad-libbed a great replacement. When not speaking, he gave his full attention to the other actors. This experience was transformative. Mike's self-confidence increased, his posture improved, and he began to initiate conversations with staff and his peers.

The power of an audience's attention is difficult to describe, but when you're standing on a stage, that power is palpable, it is overwhelming. Most of our students were never chosen to be in high school productions and never considered taking college acting classes. Providing that unique opportunity at Autistry is not only fun but is now a fundamental part of our program.

Sara helps a student with homework

LIFELONG LEARNING

As our program expands and our population ages, we envision many new educational offerings at Autistry. Being open to new perspectives, new ideas, and new experiences invigorates the brain. And that is good for everyone. One of the first questions we ask prospective staff is not "What do you know?" but "Are you willing to learn?"

Core Value #8: Never stop learning

SRIRACHA HOT
NATURAL COLOR
5001 Earle Ave.,
(626) 286-8328
NET WT. 28 OZ.

LIFE SKILLS AND CHALLENGES

We began Autistry with a focus on building creative projects to improve problem-solving and resiliency. What we discovered was that many of our students had very little experience performing day-to-day activities such as dishes, laundry, house cleaning, etc. Even before we launched the day program, we incorporated many of these activities into the Core Workshops. The students helped us prepare the lunch, set up for the lunch, and clean up after the lunch. With the day program we have the time to address these life skills more directly.

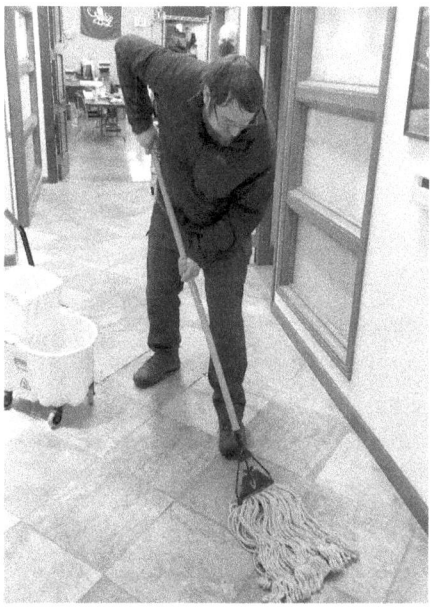

Keeping the floors clean

We now schedule cooking workshops and weekly studio janitorial chores. The students learn to prepare their favorite meals, study nutrition, and get lots of experience washing dishes. They have also taken on the janitorial chores, including cleaning the bathrooms, taking out the garbage, and mopping the floors. When we added a second studio location, the first piece of equipment we installed was a large washer and dryer so students could learn how to do laundry by washing the studio tablecloths.

IN THE KITCHEN

From the early days at the barn, midday meals were an important part of the Autistry experience. We started serving them when we realized

Finding the right pressure to break an egg

that many of our students were not eating healthy foods. Serving lunches quickly turned into making lunches together in a twist on the fish proverb: serve a student lunch and you feed them for a day, teach a student to cook lunch and they feed themselves for a lifetime.

Cooking requires skills that we often take for granted. These skills are not difficult to learn, but they do need practice. Cracking an egg is a good example. It is not difficult to do, but it does require the ability to control force. Charlie smashed several eggs into the counter on his first cooking session. He then overcompensated and tapped the eggs so gently that they didn't break at all. With practice, he found the right amount of pressure to crack the shell without the contents spilling.

Recipes provide lessons that have many out-of-kitchen applications. Following a recipe is good practice in careful reading. Details can be important. Half a teaspoon (1/2 tsp) is very different from half a tablespoon (1/2 tbsp). That "b" can be the difference between a tasty cupcake and a salty cupcake. Developing the habit of attending to details comes in handy when assembling IKEA furniture, reading a class syllabus, or following directions on a medicine bottle.

Math is an important tool when cooking, especially when doubling or halving a recipe. A recent birthday cake turned into birthday brownies when Jenny miscalculated the increase in baking powder needed to make two cakes. We took the opportunity to set up the white board and review multiplication. Math is much easier to understand when it is paired with chocolate.

Cooking also presents us with self-regulation opportunities. We all had to practice creative resiliency when we halved a chocolate pudding recipe. We were faced with the dilemma of how to divide an egg in half.

For our more rigid thinkers this was a real challenge. But we finally all agreed that a bit of extra egg would not cause a problem.

Shopping is an essential element when cooking. One of the first tasks before cracking eggs is to make a list of the ingredients needed for the recipe and to check that those ingredients are in the kitchen. With a list in hand, we can go to the grocery store, which, as it turns out, becomes a powerful learning experience, thanks to our college student interns.

Occupational Therapy (OT) interns had started working with us as a result of a visit to Autistry in 2014 by Julia Wilbarger. At that time, she was an Associate Professor in the Occupational Therapy Department at Dominican University (DU). Julia walked through the studio, exploring all the tools and the student projects as we described our program. "This is all OT—everything you are doing here is occupational therapy." So began a deeply productive relationship with DU that continues to this day. Autistry hosts OT student interns each semester, providing

> "This is all OT— everything you are doing here is occupational therapy."

Navigating the grocery store

them with numerous opportunities to create OT interventions. The interns provide Autistry with enthusiastic, innovative staff, and they keep us up to date with research in the field.

One group of DU interns saw the shopping trip as a multi-faceted OT experience. Working closely with our OT staff, the interns created a series of activities to address several skills simultaneously. The students practiced spatial awareness and driving skills as they pushed the shopping carts down the aisles. They had to be aware of other shoppers, be mindful of obstacles such as product displays, read signs to find the right location of items, and ask store staff for help.

THE PERILS OF SUGAR

In the early days of Autistry we made very sweet and very yummy chocolate brownies. We noticed that arguments would break out among the students and among the staff within an hour after eating them. We called them Fighting Brownies and now only serve them on very special outdoor occasions where there will be lots of activity to work off the sugar.

What we see in the workshops when students eat significant amounts of sugar is increased energy accompanied by fast, pressured speech and disconnected thoughts. What follows is a Sugar Crash that often looks like depression as the students have difficulty engaging in projects and are easily frustrated.

To maintain a peaceful and productive studio, we banned sugary soft drinks. Thinking we were decreasing sugar at the lunch table, we offered juices instead. What we soon realized is that fruit juice is yet another source of sugar (fructose). Many students would gravitate to the lemonade or apple juice and drink several glasses with their lunch. Again, we witnessed agitated behaviors, lack of concentration, and moodiness when we returned to work. We now serve watered-down juice (half water/half juice) and ice water at the lunch table. We also plan a physical activity after the meal to help digest our food and get our energy back. This is usually a walk to the park and an energetic game. On rainy days we do indoor exercise routines. Decreased sugar and increased physical activity have made a huge difference in post-lunch productivity.

DIET DIVERSITY

Limiting sugar was a good start. It is an easy concept to describe to the students, and the effect of eating high sugar foods is something most students have experienced and can immediately understand. Discussing sugar also opens the door to discussing diet in general.

Many of our students are on specific diets either prescribed by their doctor or adopted by their family. As discussed briefly in Chapter 1, our family has been on a gluten-free/dairy-free (GF/DF) diet since 1998. At that time, there were several articles circulating on the internet about the link between gluten, dairy, and the brain, but there were few products at the grocery store to support a gluten-free or dairy- free diet.

We first tested the diet on Dan. He decided to stop eating food with

gluten or casein (milk protein) for one week to see what would happen. Dan is a scientist by training and inclination. He is skeptical of fads and always does the research to figure out why something works the way it does. After just two days he reported surprising results. He had more energy. His sinuses were clearer, which allowed him to sleep more soundly. He also reported an improved ability to withstand sensory input (scratchy fabric, loud voices, odors). All of these results improved his mood and lessened his anxiety. Over the next several months Dan also lost 65 pounds which he has kept off to this day.

Making an omelet

Dan's success with the diet motivated us to try it with Ian, who was three years old at the time. He did not understand why he had to give up his favorite Straus organic milk, Cheerios, and Pop Tarts. He pushed back on us. He cried and threw a couple good tantrums. But we found rice milk was an acceptable replacement for dairy milk, and oatmeal replaced Cheerios for breakfast. We just had to make our own Pop Tarts using rice flour and guar gum—not the same, but they looked similar.

Ian's response to the change in diet was also positive. We had not told his teacher or the classroom aides that Ian was now on the GF/DF diet. After two weeks, we received a note from his teacher praising Ian's improved behavior. He was engaging in group activities. He was also making impressive progress in his speech and general communication ability.

At home we noted that Ian's level of agitation had decreased. He no longer hit his head against the floor when frustrated. His sleeping improved—though it would be another year or so before he slept through the night. We reported these improvements to his pediatrician and began to ease off his medications until Ian was medication free.

The GF/DF diet may not work for everyone, but our experience taught us the important role food plays in our overall health, both physical and mental. We applied this lesson to Autistry lunches. Communal lunches prepared at Autistry always include:

- GF/DF options (there are many gluten-free pastas and breads available now)
- A high protein dish—usually roast chicken but also a vegan option
- Several choices of vegetable (broccoli seems to be the most popular!)

We have also instigated a lunch policy for non-communal lunches:
- No soft drinks
- No highly processed sugary foods (candy bars)

We work with each student to understand their diet and to help them create a healthy lunch. We were surprised and very pleased when several families reported that the students were eating healthier at home too.

COMMUNITY MOBILITY TRAINING

One day, when Ian was 22, we picked him up from his house and noticed his neck was very sunburned. When we asked where he had been to get that much sun, he told us about an adventure he'd had the day before. Ian's favorite county park is about five miles outside of town. The previous day he had taken the bus from his house to the downtown transit center. There is no public transportation to McNears Beach Park, so he walked.

That seemed like a reasonable decision. He had packed some snacks that he ate at the park, sitting on the pier looking out over the bay. When he finished eating, he decided to continue north along Point San Pedro Road rather than returning to the transit station. A couple of miles north is another park, China Camp Beach. He filled his water bottle there and continued north. He walked another five miles to the Marin Civic Center. He crossed under the freeway, found a bus stop, and took a Golden Gate Transit bus back home.

By the end of Ian's story, we were proud of his courageous adventuring spirit but also dismayed that he had walked over 12 miles. We were

Yep, it says Share the Road

also concerned about his safety, so we drove him back along Point San Pedro Road and pointed out that there were no sidewalks along most of the 12 miles from the transit station to the Civic Center. We explained that he could have been hit by a car. His response was to point to a large yellow road sign. "Look. It says, 'Share the Road.'"

If only crosswalks and road signs could keep us safe! This absolute trust in road signs and street markings led us to take a deeper dive into how our students navigate through the community. We realized we had not considered the need for training in how to use the public transportation system and, even more than that, in how to navigate independently and safely within the community. We had witnessed our students neglecting to look both ways when crossing a street or failing to catch the attention of an oncoming driver when in a crosswalk. When asked, the students would often respond with "But I was in a crosswalk," as if that were protection enough against two tons of steel hurling towards them.

We reached out to Dr. Miriam Monahan, OTD OTR/L, founder and director of the Driver Rehabilitation Institute. Dr. Monahan is a licensed Occupational Therapist and world-renowned expert in the field of cognition, driving, and general urban situational awareness. She worked with Autistry staff Occupational Therapist, Benji Harrington, OTR/L to create the Autistry Community Mobility Program. The goal was to assess our students' ability to move safely around in the community whether walking, bicycling, using public transportation, or driving.

Many of our students needed help developing situational awareness.

Many of our students needed help developing situational awareness. They needed help recognizing and identifying issues as well as learning the best way to respond to those issues.

Using John Michon's hierarchical model of driving, Miriam and Benji created activities to evaluate the students' ability in the following three areas:

1. Operational: ability to manage routine situations (uses crosswalks, bus passes, and rideshare app)
2. Tactical: ability to manage unplanned events with control and on-the-spot decision making (changes route if there is an obstruction, crosses streets safely when there is no crosswalk)
3. Strategic: ability to plan the trip (gets appropriate addresses, checks a map and gets directions, knows what time to leave to arrive on schedule)

Navigating through town

The activities included walking independently to a designated destination in town using a map. Benji and Miriam would follow at a discreet distance to observe how each student navigated the route. Did they look both ways before crossing a street? Were they aware of their surroundings, other people, and vehicles?

Surprising information was revealed by these assessments. Timothy veered way off the proscribed route as he did not understand how to read a street sign. He thought that the sign parallel to the street was announcing the name of the intersecting street. It became clear to us why Timothy was so often late to workshops. What became clear to Benji was that Timothy used landmarks to navigate through town. With this information Benji was able to teach Timothy how to use Google maps street view to find the

physical landmarks he needed to guide him to his destination.

A more common issue we found was that students often looked down while they were walking and did not scan their surroundings. This was not only dangerous, leaving them vulnerable to being hit by quiet electric cars, it was a social issue. By keeping their heads down, they were not interacting with others and could seem unengaged and uninterested in their community.

This disengagement was also a problem when learning to take public transportation. Many students would become focused on their phones and miss their stop. How they dealt with this situation depended on their tactical ability—could they figure out how to get back to the stop they missed?

To reinforce the practice of paying attention while riding a bus, Benji incorporated an exercise into the bus outings: students took turns tracking the route on their phones and pulling the cord to alert the driver that the group's destination stop was coming up. When

Focusing on your phone can be dangerous

on a walking excursion where there was no sidewalk, Benji would often shout out "Hey, there's no sidewalk. What side of the road should we walk on?" Over time more students responded correctly.

A surprising moment occurred when we realized that many students did not know that the numbers listed on a bus stop refer to the bus route that stops there. They also needed to learn how and whom to ask for help, the bus driver being likely to be better informed on the bus routes than a fellow passenger sitting in the seat in front of them.

Miriam taught a Community Mobility workshop that included a section devoted to understanding and recognizing how vehicles communicate with humans. From that workshop, Benji and the Autistry staff created Car Light Jeopardy, a game that provided the answers—for example: "They flash on and off on either the right or left side of the car." The students provided the questions: "What are turn signals?" The knowledge gained by playing the game was then tested when the students were out in the community with pop quiz questions like "What do those red lights mean?" Because information left unused remains abstract, and abstract thought is often difficult for our concrete thinkers to remember or understand, this activity helped the students retain information by using it in a functional real-world setting.

Information left unused remains abstract

The Community Mobility Program is a work-in-progress as we assess and reassess our students' ability to journey independently and safely to and through their community. The assessments and observations provide information for us to use as we create new activities and new programs.

FASHION SENSE

Another plus of having college-age interns and staff is the pop culture sensibility they bring to the studio. We have several older staff members who bring wisdom and experience, but the younger staff provide a connection to the trends of the current world such as popular films, video games, fashion, and dating.

Robert, a bright, handsome twenty-something young man, was having difficulty getting social traction. He had tried dating sites, but the few face-to-face encounters he'd had would generally end with an "I'll call you" that never materialized. We practiced social communication techniques, and he had a good grasp on the verbal give and take necessary to sustain a dinner conversation. What we hadn't thought about was how Robert presented himself sartorially. His pants were too short and his T-shirts were too tight and covered in logos of outdated tv shows.

Gabrielle, a young staff member, did notice. She took Robert aside and discussed wardrobe choices with him. At her suggestion Robert brought in boxes of all of his clothing. He and Gabrielle went through the clothes piece by piece. They discarded T-shirts and pants that were hopelessly dated, too short, or too worn. They were left with a very small pile of clothes.

Together they examined Robert's finances and came up with a wardrobe budget. Then they went shopping. When they returned, we were all surprised at how much better Robert looked in his new clothes. Because we were used to Robert's old clothing choices, we had not fully registered how they made him look out of step. After a couple more unsuccessful dates, Robert finally clicked with a young woman and entered a long-term relationship. Did the new wardrobe make a difference? It certainly didn't hurt!

WORKING OUT

In the first years of Autistry workshops we recognized the importance of physical activity, especially as so many of our students spend hours sitting in front of computer screens. We would take breaks to walk around the block or do stretches to re-energize. We found that exercise is a great stress reliever. Exercise helps regulate adrenaline, the hormone released when your body feels in danger or is under stress. The effects of stress can be serious: headaches, irritability, memory loss, diarrhea, insomnia. For many of our students, everyday life is stressful, and their adrenal glands are on high alert.

Cycling off that excess energy

Caroline, an engaging, active young woman with a great sense of humor, became anxious when confronted with any new situation or task. We tried the "just work through it" approach, but that seemed to increase her anxiety level rather than abate it. We realized that Caroline did not have the ability to use deep breathing or other quiet techniques to calm herself in the moment. She needed to "work it out" not just "work through it." We set up a stationary bicycle, and whenever her anxiety became too high, she would jump on and pump the pedals for ten minutes. This worked. Caroline was able to release the pent-up adrenaline and calmly return to her work.

The lesson we learned from Caroline is the importance of cardio-vascular exercise and overall physical fitness. We incorporated fitness workouts into our program. We enrolled our students into fitness classes at the local community college, and we added yoga and stretching at the studio. The benefits were immediate. Exercise not only reduces stress hormones like adrenaline, it encourages the production of endorphins, hormones in the brain that increase feelings of pleasure and wellbeing. The students not only felt good, but they also thought more clearly and were able to manage their moods better. A definite win for everyone.

Now when we plan the college semester schedules for our students, we recommend that each student take a physical fitness class. There are several options available—–weight training, swimming, yoga, dance. This is another opportunity for peer appropriate community integration. Our students perform well in the fitness courses and are welcomed by the staff and other students.

One semester we worried when a fitness instructor approached our class mentor and said he felt students would not be able to do the exercises and would disrupt his yoga class. A class member overheard the discussion, came forward, and said, "My brother is autistic, and he does yoga every day." Other class members, many of whom had met our students in other classes, joined him in support of our students. The instructor relented and, of course, the students worked hard and did well. At the end of the semester, the instructor let us know that our students are welcome in any class he teaches. Experience had overturned his

Working out

assumptions and prejudices. This was a great example of how to change the world one person at a time.

EXERCISE IS NOT CORPORAL PUNISHMENT

Still, advocating exercise as a way to moderate or regulate behavior can be a hard sell to public institutions like schools. When Ian was in second grade, we recommended that he run the perimeter of the campus if he was having a hard time engaging with the classroom activities. He was mainstreamed at that time, but his attention span was much shorter than the other students and he would disengage frequently. The disengagement generally signaled that he was overwhelmed with information and needed a break. Fired by anxiety, Ian's adrenaline would rise, and his behavior would become inappropriate for the classroom—talking out loud to himself, rocking back and forth in his seat, or leaving his seat to move around the room.

Our suggested intervention, allowing him to run a circuit on campus was met with absolute disapproval. "That is corporal punishment," the principal told us. The administration was unswayed by our insistence that physical exercise helped Ian regulate the anxiety causing the behaviors. Full inclusion for neurodivergent individuals sounds like a wonderful idea, but unless it is accompanied by a basic understanding of the diverse needs of individuals, it can be a painful and traumatizing experience for a student. For Ian, having to remain at his school desk when his internal chemistry was driving him to move was the true corporal punishment.

CHANGE SUCKS!

As most of us who are on the spectrum or work with individuals on the spectrum know, transitions are tough. Times of transition or change are when most autistic meltdowns occur. The change can be as simple as going from one class to another, leaving the house, or taking a different route home from school. The response to the change often seems out of proportion to the size of the change. When considering the difficulty of transitions, it is important to consider that resistance to change is a normal response.

Studies show that humans are hardwired to resist change. Change can represent a threat. When faced with a perceived threat, the amygdala sends signals to the autonomic nervous system to release hormones for fight, flight, or freeze. Neurodivergent individuals often have difficulty processing information quickly, so a strong reaction to change may actually represent a survival strategy. Fight, flight, and freeze are major components of the autistic meltdown.

LEAVING THE BABY DOCTOR

One rite of passage (transition) is the move from pediatrician to adult physician. Many of our students in their early twenties still see their pediatrician or see no doctor at all. There may be several reasons for this. It can be overwhelming for a young adult to consider sharing with a new doctor the intimate details of their anatomy and their very personal health issues. The family may also be hesitant to make the change as pediatricians generally know more about and have more experience with autistics. Some doctors will not allow a parent to accompany an adult child into the examination room unless the individual is legally conserved. For some this may be appropriate, but for others, especially those with communication challenges, this can be a problem.

Many of our students in their early twenties still see their pediatrician or see no doctor at all.

We often accompany Ian into the exam room as he has difficulty describing symptoms to his doctor. After several visits, his general physician now knows to ask specific rather than open-ended questions. Rather than asking, "How does your throat feel?" she will ask "Does your throat feel dry?" "Does it hurt when you swallow?" We helped her learn how to interact with Ian to get the information she needed to help him.

Ian also misinterprets directions. Once during an internal rectal exam with a new specialist, the doctor asked Ian to "squeeze my finger." Ian immediately reached around, grabbed the doctor's finger and gave it a squeeze. The shock on the doctor's face was priceless. He didn't know whether to laugh or be angry. Janet laughed, giving him permission to laugh. The doctor then apologized for having strongly suggested that Janet stay out of the exam room.

Clear communication with medical professionals is very important. Misunderstandings and misinterpretations can lead to the prescription of the wrong medications or the wrong dosages.

Benjamin arrived at Autistry one day in a high state of anxiety. He was unable to focus or to sit still for any length of time. When questioned, he said that he had not taken his morning medication.

"The pills make me nauseous," he said. "And I don't like how they slow down my thinking."

Benjamin went on to say that even though he had seen his doctor the week before, he had not told her about the negative reaction to the medication. Benjamin's family does not live nearby, and it is not part of our program to accompany a student to medical appointments. We did help him make the appointment, and we helped him write a script that he could use when he saw his doctor. We were all a bit relieved when the doctor lowered the dosage and that seemed to alleviate the negative reactions.

> Clear communication with medical professionals is very important.

There is a great need to educate medical professionals, especially those who treat adults, in how best to communicate with neurodivergent individuals. In the meantime, we must consider providing an advocate, parent, sibling, or mentor to help those who need it to navigate the health system to get the help they need.

SCIENCE BACKS US UP

Diet, exercise, the gut—the changes we made in our lives and in the Autistry program are now backed up by science. Our Fighting Brownies demonstrated the dark side of glucose. Glucose is the main source of fuel for the brain. Glucose supports essential brain functions—thinking, memory storage and retrieval, and learning. Glucose also triggers the brain to release feel-good hormones like dopamine and endorphins, known at the Happiness Hormones. High levels of these hormones create the Sugar High.

However, the high level of glucose in the brownies caused the body to produce insulin in order to maintain a sugar balance, and that caused a sudden drop in the glucose levels. This led to the Sugar Crash. This low glucose period has many negative effects, including an inability to concentrate, reduced thinking speed, memory difficulties, and increased irritability.

The effect of exercise on mental and physical health is well researched and documented. Physical activity has been found to reduce anxiety and actually promote positive physiological change on several crucial regulating body systems. Those systems include:

- The hypothalamic-pituitary-adrenal axis (HPA) that mediates the effects of stressors by regulating metabolism
- The monoamine system that includes serotonin, dopamine, and adrenaline and helps regulate clear thinking and emotional states
- The opioid system, also referred to as the brain's reward center, contains receptors to hook up with endorphins and cause the release of dopamine—the feel-good neurotransmitter.

Taking dietary habits seriously is now backed up by scientific research. Current research is discovering a strong relationship between the brain and the gut. It is a bilateral relationship: the brain affects the gut, and the gut affects the brain. Most of us have experienced the feeling of nausea or upset tummy caused by unpleasant or fearful thoughts. But we often overlook the moments when a tummy ache causes sluggish thinking.

Scientists have found that the gut microbiome, which consists of trillions of microorganisms (fungi, viruses, yeast, bacteria), plays a large role in brain

Exercising to reduce anxiety

health. These microorganisms interact with the central nervous system and influence the brain systems that regulate stress, anxiety, and memory. These are the very areas we found improved with a careful diet.

Studies show that the gut microbiome produces 90 percent of the body's serotonin whereas the brain only produces 10 percent. Serotonin regulates your mood. SSRIs (selective serotonin reuptake inhibitors) are often prescribed as antidepressants to increase serotonin levels in the brain.

For decades, individuals suffering from depression and other mental health issues have been told "It is all in your head." Now we are beginning to understand that it is also in our gut. This is a new field of research but one that we are watching with interest and hope.

Core Value #9: Healthy living
involves the body and the brain

CHAPTER 10

VOCATIONAL PARTNERSHIPS

When we began offering Build Stuff Workshops in 2008 for autistics transitioning from high school to the adult world, we modeled the workshops after group therapy sessions—small cohorts meeting once a week for a period of eight to ten weeks. We envisioned starting new groups every couple of months. That is not what happened. When the eight weeks were over, the students kept coming. Many are still with us nearly 15 years later.

There were several factors contributing to the extended timeframe: the projects were generally more complex and took longer than eight weeks to complete, the students needed extensive training to learn and master the new skills necessary to create the projects, and there were no other programs available for them. But the strongest reason for creating ongoing workshops was the overwhelming desire of the students to return to a place where they felt understood and where they could get the support they needed for their creative ventures.

> If these bright, talented individuals were going to stay with us long-term, we needed to help them become independent adults

For us this new timeline meant thinking well beyond the traditional group therapy model—it meant creating a community of sustained support. If these bright, talented individuals were going to stay with us long-term, we needed to help them become independent adults, to develop strong marketable skills, and to prepare them to navigate the neurotypical world. This required creating a "community integration" program.

How we earn a living is not only how we participate in our community, but it is, in large measure, how we define ourselves. We needed to reach outside our comfortable Autistry bubble and develop working relationships with potential employers to find viable opportunities for our students. The CORE Workshops had shown us that our students could learn vocational skills by building personal projects. But it is a very different mindset to use those skills for the benefit of an employer. We continue to offer Build-Stuff Workshops and Tinker Workshops to develop skills, but for learning about work and

Ready for work

how to work, we realized that the best place is at work.

We looked at the job placement programs that were available and noted that most were based on partnerships with large corporations—Safeway, Google, Salesforce, etc. These companies had several entry-level positions they could offer to supported-employment programs, and for those who were interested in these placements, the programs worked well. But when we discussed these job opportunities with our students we were met with blank stares or, more commonly, the response of "I'm not interested in grocery stores" or "I don't like offices."

Begin with environments that contain objects or activities of personal interest.

Anyone who has worked with individuals on the autism spectrum, or anyone who is autistic, knows that there is no one more stubborn than an autistic. If they do not want to do something or are not interested, they will dig in their heels up to their knees. When exploring possible work placements, it is best to begin with environments that contain objects or activities of personal interest.

CHOO-CHOO TO THE RESCUE

Trains seem to be a common interest among our students. We had experienced this with Ian and his love of Thomas the Tank Engine. As we met more autistics, we met more train enthusiasts. A quick Google search of Autism + Trains will return a long list of articles exploring this phenomenon. The reasons given are generally: there is an attraction to spinning objects (wheels), trains are easily organized by type and model

(order), they go directly from one point to another on a designated track (predictable), and the sound of a train is well-modulated and calming.

Whatever the reason, trains seem to be of great interest to many of our students.

When Ian was seven years old, we took him to the Western Railway Museum. Usually when Ian visited public attractions, even zoos filled with cool animals, he would be found in the parking lot, examining the inanimate tires of parked cars. The Western

Trains at the Western Railroad Museum

Railway Museum totally engaged him. He toured each car house, ran his hands along each train, and listened with reverence as the conductor of the train ride described the railway history. Ian was definitely in his element, as was Dan, who also has a childhood love of trains.

The mission of this unique facility, run by the Bay Area Electric Railroad Association, is to preserve the regional heritage of electric railway transportation. This entails encouraging the public's interest in trains with informative and engaging

Working in the restoration shop

displays while maintaining the growing collection of streetcars, interurban cars, and mainline railroad cars as well as electric, steam, and diesel locomotives. Located about an hour north of the Autistry studio, the museum grounds have over 22 miles of railroad track once a part of the historic Sacramento Northern mainline. The expansive undertaking of the museum is made possible by the support of a small, dedicated staff and more than 125 volunteers.

As we researched possible vocational training sites, we were reminded of how excited Ian was by the Western Railway Museum trains. Dan and Ian went out for a visit and spent some time working in the Restoration Shop where the museum equipment is maintained and restored. Dan and Ian continued to visit often and worked out the possibility of bringing a crew of Autistry students out to work there. This was the start of a

Cleaning train parts

strong, long-term partnership. There is an endless amount of work to be done restoring the historic trolley cars, maintaining the museum and the grounds, and engaging with the public. The museum always needs more volunteers to help get their work done. It is a rewarding place for our students to intern. Our crews work alongside the Museum staff and volunteers, and Autistry students have become an important part of the Western Railroad Museum family.

We have developed plans for several tracks of work in various areas of the museum. The tasks include:

- Collecting fees and checking membership cards at the entrance
- Cashiering and reshelving items in the bookstore
- Serving and cleaning up at the snack bar
- Digitizing the collection of documents and photos in the extensive museum archive
- Grounds maintenance
- Working as docents, assisting visitors, and explaining the history and technology of the exhibits

Learning how to drive the train

For some of our students, becoming operators of the equipment and working in the restoration shop are excellent long-term occupations.

We continue to be surprised and have learned to value the experience of working with our students in new environments. There have been many lessons learned working with the students at Western Railway Museum. It was a lesson to us of just how much coordination is required to simply sweep a very cluttered area, like the shop. Sliding a broom across the floor seems like a very easy task, but when the activity is broken down into its various actions, it is not so simple. One must apply gentle downward pressure on the broom to keep it in contact with the floor. Sweeping the broom requires a cross-body motion involving both sides of the body in coordination. At the end of the sweeping stroke, care must be taken to apply the correct amount of force to keep the collected materials from flying into the air.

Sam presented us with an excellent example of the challenge of sweeping. He is a wiz on the computer. He touch-types, and he maneuvers the mouse around with ease. A casual observer would assume that he had good eye/hand coordination. But that ease of motion did not translate to sweeping the floor of the train shed.

Sam has difficulty with body movements that cross the midline, the vertical center line of the body running from the top of the head through the pelvis (referred to as cross-lateral movement). Crossing that vertical center happens when one reaches across the body with an outstretched arm to grab the cereal box off the top shelf or with a leg to kick a ball to a teammate—or when sweeping a floor.

When movement crosses the midline, both brain hemispheres are activated and coordinate the movement. That right brain/left brain communication is important for coordination and cognition. This explains why, when we tried to give Sam verbal instructions on how to sweep, we were met with the deer-in-the-headlights look. He was not able to process the information and coordinate his limbs.

The only way Sam was able to learn to sweep was by repetition. It was as if he had to train each muscle and nerve to perform the activity of sweeping. But, over time, he mastered it.

Like at the Autistry wood shop, there are areas at the Railroad Museum that need awareness and training to safely navigate. Our students enjoy the daily safety briefs where we walk around the museum in our steel toed boots and high visibility vests and talk about how to walk around the tracks and equipment safely. Many of the pieces of equipment have scaffolding that has to be climbed

Lots of restoring to do on this one!

up to do work. We worked with students to climb a ladder, move from the ladder to the scaffold, and return. It is nearly universal for our students (and some staff!) to have some difficulty with these movements. One student, Ben, could very confidently and smoothly climb up and get onto the scaffold, but he was then completely unable to coordinate the movements to get down. He did manage it finally, but that led us to design a more graduated series of climbing tasks and movements to develop these skills.

The Western Railway Museum is an example of the kinds of partnerships we look for: an organization with a worthy mission that has significant volunteer labor needs and offers rich learning and occupational opportunities.

HORSES WITH ATTITUDE

Our next vocational partner, Joell Dunlap, simply knocked on our door. Joell is the founder/CEO of Square Peg Foundation, an organization based in Half Moon Bay (south of San Francisco) that offers adaptive

horse-riding programs for individuals with learning and/or developmental disabilities and at the same time provides a new life for retired thoroughbred racehorses. In August of 2018, Joell launched a satellite program near Autistry. She introduced herself and her program to neighboring

Joell Dunlap, founder of Square Peg Foundation

like-minded organizations, and Autistry was first on her visitation list.

Little did Joell know that when she knocked on our door, she was offering the fulfillment of Sara Gardner's dream. Sara, our Autistry Clinical Director, is a lifelong equestrian. At her initial job interview, Sara told us her goal was to combine her work with autistics and her love of horses. Over the years we had tried several times to create a therapeutic equestrian program, but we just didn't have the resources to support it. With Sara in the lead, Autistry could do much more than simply participate in Joell's program—we could become a true partner.

The program Sara created at Cadence Farm in Sonoma was immediately a hit with many Autistry students. Sara quickly saw the benefits for the students as they worked at the numerous chores at Cadence Farm. The students clean the stalls, replace old straw bedding with

Team work

clean bedding, rake and clean the large training area, and wash and groom the horses. Beneath the simple manual chores, a multitude of invisible skills are being developed.

Most of us take for granted our smooth movement through space. We unconsciously scan the sidewalk ahead for possible obstacles, and we calculate the distance our arm must travel to reach that cookie tempting us on the kitchen table. Without thinking we also send the appropriate signals to our muscles, so they move in coordination and we do not trip on the sidewalk or knock the cookie onto the floor. (This spatial/ body awareness is called proprioception, a word you don't hear often unless you are an occupational therapist.) Many of us have had the experience of picking up what we thought was a full milk carton and, before

Lots of stalls to clean

we realized it was actually almost empty, nearly tossing the carton into the air. Our spatial/body expectation did not match the reality of the situation. If we are not getting clear messages from our muscles that let our brain know where our body is in space, we will experience these milk carton moments randomly throughout the day. We have found that the best way to improve the messaging from muscles to brain is to provide a variety of opportunities for mind/muscle coordination. As we learned from Sam, competency in one environment doesn't necessarily translate to a different one. Though his mind/muscle coordination seemed fluid at the keyboard, it took many days of repetitive sweeping for Sam to master that task.

> Cleaning a stall from start to finish is a true stretch of executive functioning skill.

At Cadence Farm the students get many opportunities to learn and practice new skills. One of the primary tasks of Autistry students working at Cadence is cleaning stalls. This sounds like one task, but it is actually a combination of multiple challenging tasks rolled into one. Just replacing the bedding includes using a checklist to discover what stalls need bedding, with a partner filling a wheelbarrow with bedding, bringing it to a stall, and dumping and spreading the bedding in the correct place. Cleaning a stall from start to finish is a true stretch of executive functioning skill. It involves multiple complex motor movements and

many opportunities for decision making, communication, and judgment. It also presents multiple sensory challenges that the students are willing to take on because they care about the work they are doing. Over the months, our students have continued to gain skills and confidence.

Every day, horses are led to pastures and paddocks from their stalls and back again. This involves safely approaching and haltering a horse.

The student must also find and return each horse to a specific stall. It is very important for the student to communicate with the horse, being clear about what they are asking the horse to do and setting firm boundaries. It is an opportunity for leadership that our students do not have enough of in their lives, and they rise

Taking the horse back to the barn

to the challenge. Each student is met at their level and challenged at the pace that is right for them. Different skills, aptitudes, and personalities are taken into consideration when matching horses and handlers.

Equine communication and training is taken to the next level as students add hand-walking, lunging, and round-pen work into their repertoire. Both in the round-pen and in lunging, students work the horses around them in a circle with the use of a lunge whip. This complicated task is broken down into small elements. The students work with

experienced horse trainers to learn the various cues to give the horses (walk, trot, canter). They also learn to read a horse's emotional and physical state by observing his movement and body language. Are the horse's ears pointed forward, signifying that he is engaged with you? Or are

Deep conversation

his ears flattened back indicating anger or aggression? Is his head lowered and relaxed, or is it held high, alerted to something in the distance or possibly indicating the horse is in pain? Learning how to read a horse is great training in how to read a person.

The students show incredible empathy for their horse partners as well as pride in the work they are doing to provide healing and quality of life. One of Cadence's elder horses, Luke, truly had a vastly improved quality of life during his last year because of Autistry students' regular and dedicated care.

One regular task at Cadence Farm is cleaning and organizing the grain room. We also sometimes help with unloading grain and very occasionally have made the run to the feed store to pick up needed tools and grain. Students also regularly tidy the tack room and clean and condition leather gear such as saddles and bridles. All these tasks are excellent real-world opportunities to improve executive functioning skills (planning, organizing, etc.) as well as the development of fine motor skills.

One of our mentors once referred to one of the horses as her "horsie boyfriend." Since then, a number of students have named their own "horsie" boyfriend, girlfriend, or BFF. Mentors and Cadence staff know the horse or horses each student gravitates toward, and they try to pair

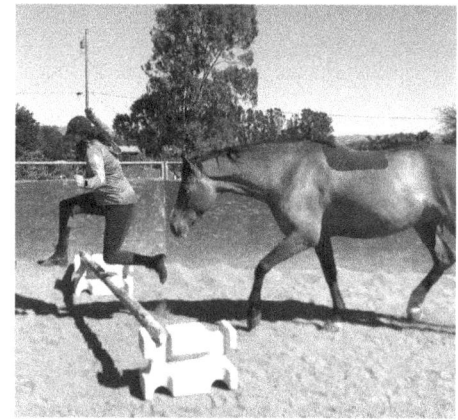

"Do it like this!"

them whenever possible. These pairings are not always predictable or obvious, with some reserved students showing a connection to an especially feisty young racehorse or an energetic student preferring to work with one of our elder horses. Each horse has many specific things to teach and to learn. As is true in all aspects of Autistry, this teaching and learning is founded on relationships.

Working at the barn is an incredibly dynamic environment. While there are routines, they are constantly shifting. Turn-out assignments

(taking horses from their stalls) change with new horses arriving or adjusting to an injury or illness. The latch on almost every gate in the barn works in a slightly different way. Each halter has differences in its material, weight, and fit. Students are challenged to learn skills and routines that can be adjusted as needed.

Understanding communication in its many forms is imperative to getting through the day. Tasks are listed on a whiteboard but may shift throughout the day. If a student is working with a partner, communication is required in small moments such as negotiating which part of the stall to work in or in deciding when and how to bring the manure bucket to dump in the tractor. There are also natural opportunities for nuanced communication, such as reporting a horse that needs medical attention, asking for help, and assigning tasks.

Casey is a student who came to us with a low frustration tolerance threshold and an often grumpy or disinterested demeanor. But animals were a subject that could bring a smile to Casey's face. He took great pride in noticing and identifying wild animals on Autistry hikes and enjoyed finding and showing amazing or amusing animal videos on YouTube. Casey has tremendous pride in his aptitude for noticing details others have missed and for creative problem-solving. At Cadence, Casey keeps a keen eye out for sources of danger, from pulling small scraps of metal out of the pastures to noting fences in need of mending.

A combination of these talents as well as the level of horsemanship Casey has developed were revealed when Casey found Danny, an older gray Connemara Arabian cross, straddling a fence with his back legs in the pasture and his front legs out. Casey immediately ran to get Danny's halter and assist him through the fence and back to the stall. He then went to the barn manager to tell him that the other horses were not safe in that pasture until the fence could be repaired. He helped the barn manager bring the rest of the horses back to their stalls and pointed out the area of the fence that he determined to be the source of the problem. All this required a tremendous combination of agency, discernment, communication, and horsemanship skills, and Casey was rightly proud.

A couple of months later, "Dublin Dave," a Square Peg employee, told Sara he was going to try to repair an arena gate that was hanging at the wrong angle. Sara asked if he would bring Casey with him and he happily agreed. Casey examined the problem and developed a plan. Dave allowed him a leadership role, and Casey fulfilled that role to everyone's satisfaction and benefit. When Dave returned, he said that working with Casey on the gate reminded him of his construction days working with an experienced foreman.

Creative problem-solving is a universally beneficial life skill that many autistic students excel at. Work at the barn provides natural and meaningful opportunities to refine this skill while developing the communication skills that allow for sharing information and asking for help, both essential for problem-solving to be useful and effective.

Bath day!

With the large variety of tasks and skills, there is tremendous opportunity for visible growth. What this often looks like is a drastic increase in independence. Almost all students initially required hand-over-hand assistance to learn how to put a halter on a horse. A student feels immense pride having gone from needing help putting a tine through a hole to buckle a halter to walking into a paddock, opening and closing the gate behind them, identifying the horse they need to get, approaching that horse in a safe way that does not cause it to retreat, and communicating with the horse to independently halter it and lead it back out the gate. Our students get a meaningful confidence and identity-affirming boost when they master tasks that the majority of neurotypical people do not know how to do.

OPEN SPACES, OPEN HEARTS

We often receive donations of tools, art supplies, materials of all sorts at Autistry. One day we opened the door to find a uniformed woman standing in front of a stack of boxes and bags. She was a park ranger who had been cleaning her hobby closet. She brought us yards of wonderfully

diverse fabrics—mostly cotton quilting material. This was a much-appreciated donation as small quilts are great first sewing projects. Sewing is almost a lost art, but it is a great exercise in planning and eye-hand coordination, and, oddly enough, it is good training for learning how to drive. The sewing machine pedal is not unlike the gas pedal in a car. The gentle shifting of foot pressure creates great muscle

Our students get a meaningful confidence and identity-affirming boost when they master tasks that the majority of neurotypical people do not know how to do.

memory that can be useful when a person gets behind the wheel. We have done several cool quilt projects at Autistry and, with the ranger's donation, we will be able to do many more.

Riding with the ranger at Marin County Park

Ranger Haimovitch's visit also opened the door to another great partnership. As we sorted through the fabulous fabric that she brought, we talked about the extensive and diverse park system in Marin. The Marin County Parks Service oversees 17,900 acres of incredibly beautiful land. The rangers maintain 39 parks, including beaches along the Pacific Ocean, lakes, lagoons, marshes, and creeks, as well as grasslands, mountains, forests of historic redwood trees, and 34 open space preserves. The rangers oversee the maintenance of hundreds of miles of hiking trails, bike paths and horse trails. Ranger Haimovitch described an endless need for volunteer help and a wide range of skill-building tasks.

This conversation led to a meeting with the volunteer program coordinator, Ranger Kirk Schroeder. Together we designed a Paid Internship Program for our students. The students work for several weeks at one park and then move to another park, working with several different rangers and gaining a wide range of experience. The initial idea was to send Autistry crews out in succession such that when one crew moved to the next park a new crew took their place. This went very well. The students enjoyed the work and learned about native plants, fence mend-

Beautiful day to work at the park

ing, and how to recognize the ever-invasive broom and acacia plants. It was hard, sweaty work, and the students learned some lessons in self-care, that wearing gloves and drinking water is important.

BEST LAID PLANS

The paid internship programs with our three partners were very popular and very successful. The students were learning new skills and developing strong work habits. With

Pulling weeds – a never-ending job

these new activities and our already strong tinker workshops and academic programs Autistry was poised to expand. We hired new staff and began to interview new students.

And then ... COVID-19.

Core Value #10: Partner with organizations with a strong community mission and range of skill-building opportunities

CHAPTER 11
COVID-19

Autistry flew into 2020 as if launched from a child's slingshot, but we were soon grounded like naughty teenagers.

In January, we were presented with the Heart of Marin Award for Excellence in Innovation. This award is given by the Center for Volunteer and Nonprofit Leadership (CVNL) to organizations in Marin County. There are more than 1,800 nonprofit organizations in Marin, and CVNL receives hundreds of nominations in each of their categories. Autistry had been nominated several times, and each year we were passed over. But this year, 2020, CVNL recognized our unique programs and highlighted our innovative approach to services to support the neurodiverse community. We were surprised and honored.

Janet and Dan receive the 2020 Bay Area Jefferson Award

In February 2020, we won a San Francisco Bay Area Jefferson Award, and we were featured on the local CBS station. The Jefferson Award Foundation (now called Multiplying Good) was founded by Jacqueline Kennedy Onassis, Senator Robert Taft, Jr, and Samuel Beard to recognize, honor, and support individuals making a difference in their community. The local CBS reporters actually visited the studio and Cadence Farm to film us at work. They interviewed an Autistry student and spent time exploring the studio and the many student projects on display. The response to the short video when it aired was strong and positive. Our phone rang steadily for days, and we were overwhelmed with the task of returning messages. After twelve years of working quietly, developing programs and services for our autistic/neurodiverse community, we were ready to expand.

Since the vendorization by Golden Gate Regional Center in 2017, we had built a robust program. The weekly schedule for each of our 22 students included college level classes, many of them at the College of Marin (COM), creative makerspace workshops, and internships with the horses at Cadence Farm, the trains at the Western Railway Museum, or the rangers of the Marin County Parks. On Fridays, we organized excursions to explore cultural and recreational activities in our community.

An example of a weekly schedule for one of our students:

Spring 2020

	MONDAY	TUESDAY	WEDNESDAY	THURSDAY	FRIDAY
9:00					
9:30		Class Prep	Maker	Class Prep	
10:00	Cadence		Workshop		Community
10:30	Farm	TO COM		TO COM	Exploration
11:00		PSYC 110		PSYC 110	Excursions
11:30		Psychology		Psychology	
12:00		11:10 - 12:30	Lunch	11:10 - 12:30	
12:30		Lunch	at Studio	Lunch	
1:00		at COM	Homework	at COM	
1:30			at		
2:00		Social Time	Studio	Social Time	
2:30					
3:00	To Transit	To Transit	To Transit	To Transit	To Transit

In March of 2020, our powerful upward trajectory stalled. We had been watching the reports of Covid as it spread across the country and through our county.

On St. Patrick's Day, March 17, 2020, we received an all-caps notice from the Marin County Health Department: **ORDER OF THE HEALTH OFFICER OF THE COUNTY OF MARIN DIRECTING ALL INDIVIDUALS LIVING IN THE COUNTY TO SHELTER AT THEIR PLACE OF RESIDENCE EXCEPT THAT THEY MAY**

**LEAVE TO PROVIDE OR RECEIVE CERTAIN ESSENTIAL SER-
VICES OR ENGAGE IN CERTAIN ESSENTIAL ACTIVITIES AND
WORK FOR ESSENTIAL BUSINESSES AND GOVERNMENTAL
SERVICES.**

We made a successful argument to the county officials and to the
Regional Center that Autistry provides essential services. We were allowed to continue operations, but the rules and directives from the various licensing organizations, the County Health Department, Golden
Gate Regional Center, and Community Care Licensing (CCL) were confusing and conflicting. It was apparent that no one knew how to handle
this novel situation.

For example, Community Care Licensing required only staff members be vaccinated. The Regional Center recommended all program
participants be vaccinated. We made it a policy that everyone, staff and
students, be vaccinated. That was easier to track and safer.

The agencies also had conflicting requirements for masking: just indoors vs indoors and outdoors. We opted for indoor/outdoor masking
by all participants at all times. Again, easier to manage and safer.

The underlying message from all the agencies was for service organizations to "Do the best you can to keep your staff and clients safe."

Autistry met the challenge head on. We gathered our bright, creative, tech-savvy staff together and made a plan to continue services
online. We initially thought that the lockdown would be a short-term
situation—maybe a few weeks. How wrong we were! Our short-term
solutions became the new normal as the lockdown continued.

Our first action was to set up an online base so that we could keep
our community together remotely. We considered several platforms
developed for businesses including Slack, Windows Team, and Google
Workspace. Then we considered our staff and students, many of whom
played online games and did not feel comfortable in the corporate online environments.

We chose Discord as our community hub. Discord was created by
a group of online gamers as a way for game developers to communicate
with each other. It launched in 2015 but expanded quickly from a place
to "Chat for Gamers" to a place to "Chat for Communities and Friends."
In early 2020, Discord upgraded their website to accommodate the

non-gaming population searching for an online home. They expanded just in time for Autistry.

ALL ABOARD FOR ONLINE

We quickly learned that although many of our students played online games, that experience didn't necessarily translate into general computer ability nor were their computer skills strong enough to overcome the effects of Covid-induced anxiety.

Terry is a young man who has always suffered from working memory impairment, an inability to retain and use information on a current task or activity. We had found that the best way for Terry to learn a new task was through continued repetition. He eventually learned new skills, but it took a long time. Terry, like many of our students, was very anxious about Covid. His already poor working memory soon became practically non-functioning. Matt, an Autistry mentor, worked with Terry to help him learn how to log in to the Discord Hub.

Matt's method of working with Terry was one we used with many students. As Terry had difficulty following directions in real time (working memory issue), Matt asked for permission to access Terry's computer directly. This allowed Terry to watch while Matt performed the necessary procedures for login. Every morning Matt would log in remotely from Terry's computer and then log out so that Terry could execute the keystrokes himself. It was a slow process, but after two weeks of daily login help Terry finally connected to the online community independently.

Taking over the command of a student's computer is similar to performing the occupational therapist's strategy of "hand over hand prompting." This is a technique that is used sparingly, as it takes control away from the student. The therapist literally moves the student's hands. However, on a physical level, hand over hand prompting can help kick-start muscle memory. When the brain is having difficulty functioning due to anxiety, communicating directly with the body can be very effective.

Studies have found a strong correlation between anxiety and cognitive functioning. Our experience with students during this stressful time totally supports those findings. The Covid years were traumatic for all our students. It was the stuff of horror films—an unseen enemy, an invisible threat in the air and on surfaces. All strangers were possible carriers of disease. With no firm data, no definitive rules, and no strong leadership, our neurodivergent students, like people everywhere, felt a deep insecurity and a growing paranoia.

FRESH AIR AND FRESH PERSPECTIVE

Some of our students live in group homes. These are homes with five to six residents who require significant support and generally have very strict rules regarding exposure to colds, viruses, or other communicable diseases. Those students were on lock-down and given permission to leave their homes only for very specific and supervised activities. Other

students developed a strong fear of exposure to Covid and did not want to leave their house. The prolonged isolation, lack of exercise, and limited fresh air increased anxiety. Many of our students regressed to behaviors we had not seen in years—not responding to texts or phone calls, unregulated emotions of anger, nail-biting, hair-pulling, and, in some cases, more serious self-harm—cutting.

Hiking through neighborhood park

This was a situation that we could not ignore. We drew a map showing the location of each of our students' homes. We organized small cohorts of students by neighborhoods. We then sent a mentor to meet up with each of the small groups, no more than four or five students. Wearing masks and keeping a safe distance from each other, the groups walked through the neighborhoods. They discovered trails, parks, and hilltops with great views. The fresh air, walking, and communicating with their peers was an enormous help in fending off depression. The hikes were so popular they are still part of our program.

Hiking in the hills

In the nearly two years of on and off shutdown we learned a lot about ourselves, our staff, and our students. Changing how we delivered service gave us some insight into the way we work. We realized when we began to hold online workshops that most of our in-person sessions were shaped by the immediate interests and moods of our students. We often laughed about how we just had to stay a couple steps ahead of the students, which meant anticipating where their creative fancies might take them and having the required tools and materials ready. This on-the-fly support allowed the students to explore their own personal ideas rather than following a set of directions. Without access to the extensive array of power tools, hand tools, wood, fabric, paints, glues, and all sorts of other resources, the Autistry mentors found they had to create another way to support project-based workshops.

A tower made of found objects

The solution was found-object projects. We put together tool kits containing scissors, tape, small glue guns, and a selection of paints and delivered them to each house. Then we asked the students to collect various household objects and lay them out on their desks in front of their computer cameras. Their collections of toilet paper rolls, feathers, egg cartons, aluminum cans, dog chewy toys and all kinds of broken toy parts led to some fantastic and strange creations: robots, castles, a theater set, and a purple monster. Many students remarked that this was a great rainy day activity that they could do at home independently. Had we not been on lockdown, this activity would not have occurred to us.

REMOTE MEANS EVERYWHERE IS CLOSE BY

Another unforeseen benefit of the Covid years was the deepening of our relationship with Fordham University in New York. We had very successfully hosted a Fordham social work student for her required work experience internship. She lived locally and was enrolled in the online Master's degree program. When Covid caused most support service agencies to close, Fordham reached out to us to see if we were offering any remote activities. By this time, we had created a full five-day program that included online college classes, social games, creative projects, and online counseling. We realized that as long as we were all online we could actually be logging in from anywhere. We took on five Fordham interns located throughout the country: Alaska, New York, Florida, Michigan, and Southern California. The remote interns added a wealth of opportunity for our students to vicariously explore new cities and to ask a thousand questions:

As we were all online, we could actually be logging in from anywhere

"Have you seen a bear?"
"Do you go to Broadway shows?"
"Are there alligators near you?"

Rebecca Foust teaches online poetry class

The interns also helped our staff provide support for students taking online classes. For some students the online experience was overwhelming. Working closely with the Student Accessibility Services at College of Marin, we were able to get logins for our mentors to attend the classes with the students. The mentors were able to take notes and also do breakout sessions if the student needed some downtime.

Staring at a screen while listening to a professor give a long lecture can be difficult for anyone. For our students with language processing issues and limited attention spans, the experience can be brutal. Before classes began, the lead mentor for each class contacted the professors to set up a pull-out system for when our students became overwhelmed. They also worked out a help signal with the students so as not to disrupt the class.

RAIN, SHINE, OR COVID

Caring for the horses

Trains and parks can take care of themselves, but horses need to be fed. During the height of the pandemic, we suspended our paid internship programs at the Western Railway Museum and with the county parks. Both venues were closed to the public at that time anyway. But we continued to work at Cadence Farm, grooming, feeding, and exercising the horses. This was an important lesson for our students (and actually for all of us): animals in your care are your responsibility regardless of weather or pandemics.

Transportation was the main problem for keeping the Cadence program open. Before Covid we drove to Cadence together in the Autistry vans or with private staff vehicles. When the pandemic hit, we instigated a policy whereby the students' family or their house-staff drove them to Cadence. This was inconvenient for everyone, but most every family understood and complied.

The Cadence staff set up a handwashing and temperature-taking station for everyone to use upon arrival. The students were vigilant about wearing their masks and maintaining a six-foot distance from others during the workday. Continuing to work with the horses not only helped the horses but gave the Autistry students and staff a much-needed sense of normalcy in this very abnormal time. They had a purpose that allowed them to turn their focus away from the constraints and concerns of Covid and concentrate on caring for these strong, vibrant creatures. Days spent with the horses at Cadence Farm calmed anxiety better than any medication.

> Days spent with the horses at Cadence Farm calmed anxiety better than any medication.

KEEPING TRACK

Like schools and many other government supported organizations, Autistry is primarily funded by the fees of the participant when they attend—the funds follow the client. It is essential that accurate attendance records are maintained. When the programs are in-person that is an easy task—one simply counts heads and gets on with the activities. When we transitioned to an online day program, we needed to account for attendance, but we also wanted to track engagement. It went against our principles to simply mark down that a student had logged in without interacting with them.

The staff came up with The Question of the Day. This is a practice we continue today when, due to

Great to be outside!

bad weather or a virus scare, we revert to remote services. We make it a requirement that each student answer the question posted in the Day Program channel of Autistry's Discord Hub. The questions range from "Who would you cast as the next James Bond?" to "What time period in history (so, not now!) would you most want to live in?" The questions provide an entry point for the students each morning. They also serve as great conversation starters. Once we have everyone in the hub, we can create the breakout rooms to accommodate various activities.

With our creative, young, and diverse staff we were able to create a range of interesting, fun, and educational programs. We started an

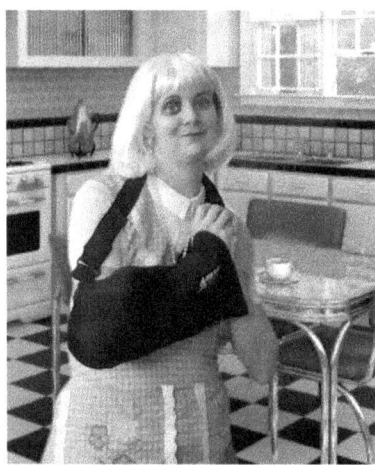

online book club where we read a book together and discussed it. Initially this was one large group, but as the reading levels of our students varied, we found it necessary to split into several smaller groups based on reading level and reading interest. The book clubs proved to be great preparation for college English and Humanity courses. The students wrote response papers and analyzed themes. They learned to identify the influences that change

Online drama class—perfect '50's look

a character and to break down the basic three-act structure of most stories. By the end of summer, they were writing short essays about the readings and even their own short stories.

One class we offered that summer was an online drama course. We had very low expectations for this as the very nature of theater or film is the interaction between characters. We found that the students excelled at performing monologues. They each created a backdrop to set the scene of their monologue, and they diligently practiced diction and delivery. Each stu-

Virtual glamour

dent found that place within themselves that resonated with their character. Their performances far exceeded our expectations. Online drama classes are not our preferred way to offer theater courses, but they offer the students an opportunity that they otherwise would not have had. The next year, when the drama students presented *A Christmas Carol*, the actor playing the narrator was unable to make the performance. We knew exactly what to do: have him participate remotely.

By summer of 2020 the programs were entirely online and an individual student's schedule could look like this:

Summer 2020					
	MONDAY	TUESDAY	WEDNESDAY	THURSDAY	FRIDAY
9:00	Question of day	Question of day	Question of day	Question of day	Question of day
9:30					
10:00		Autistry	Online	Autistry	
10:30	CADENCE	English	Art	English	Virtual
11:00		Online	Course	Online	Excursion
11:30					
12:00		Lunch	Lunch	Lunch	
12:30		& Yoga	& Yoga	& Yoga	
1:00		12-1:30	12-1:30	12-1:30	
1:30		Social	Social	Social	
2:00		Zoom	Zoom	Zoom	
2:30					

In June 2021, the Covid lockdown began to ease, and we were allowed to return to in-person programming. Again, the various oversight agencies provided conflicting guidelines. All agencies required Covid testing if staff or participants were exposed to the virus. But they did not agree on how long an exposed person should be kept isolated from others (i.e., not attend the program). The range of requirements was wide, from only 5 days for one agency to 10 days for another. By the fall of 2021, all agencies agreed that exposed individuals needed to immediately isolate for five days. If non-symptomatic after five days, they could return to the program. If they had symptoms—coughing, fever, sore throat, etc.—they needed to remain isolated for at least 10 days and they needed to be clear of symptoms before returning to the program.

No one liked these restrictions, but no one caught Covid at Autistry

Autistry started back with very small groups in short workshops. Everyone wore masks. Everyone was tested regularly for the virus and had to take their temperature before entering the studio. We no longer cooked together, and we all ate outdoors seated far apart from each other. No one liked these restrictions, but no one caught Covid at Autistry.

SHARING INFO AND INSIGHTS

We stayed together mainly via Zoom throughout the Covid years. Not only did we keep all our students, we gained some. To monitor student needs and progress, staff meetings became very important.

In the early days back at the barn, this began as a way to unwind. We would hang out together with our staff, all two of them, after the students left. We would have noticed different behaviors and different issues. As we shared our thoughts, we realized that we each had a different perspective on the students' workshop experience and that those perspectives were valuable.

These after-hours hangouts became our Clinical Session. As the staff and student numbers have increased by a factor of 10 over the years, these sessions have become crucial. We reserve at least 45 minutes at the end of every day to discuss issues that have arisen and to share thoughts on the most effective way to support our students. We share what works and what doesn't work. Our staff now includes experienced psychotherapists, occupational therapists, artists, writers, actors, woodworkers, and scientists. Each person brings a unique vision to Autistry. Taken together, the varying views and insights helped us understand our students in a more holistic, multi-dimensional way.

In a very counter-intuitive way, going virtual has kept us together.

The Covid years required the ability to communicate online, and this skill has made it possible for us to maintain Clinical Sessions while offering off-site activities. At the end of the day, a staff member can log in from their parked car after a day with students at college or from the tack room at Cadence or the library of the Western Railway Museum. In a very counter-intuitive way, going virtual has kept us together.

The Covid years also caused us to explore the future of Autistry. We asked ourselves: what type of ongoing support does our son and our students need?

Core Value #11: Staying safe does not
rule out creative growth

CHAPTER 12

THE MAKER INCUBATOR

Our original plan was to offer eight-week Project-Based Therapy Workshops, but the Friday after the end of the first workshop series, there was a knock at our door. When we opened the door, we found our students ready to go to work on projects.

"The workshop's over."

"Yeah, but we aren't done yet."

No kidding. Fifteen years later many of our original students are still with us. They are still not done.

TAKING A LONGER VIEW

From our once-a-week meetings we saw the need to do more and more often, so we developed the day program. The day program was a good start. It provided a full week of vocational training, academic pursuit, and recreational activities. But after a few years, we felt there was something missing. Where does all this lead? Some, but really only a few, of our students transitioned into mainstream jobs ranging from janitorial positions to software development. They were in the minority, as most of our students either did not want to work in the neurotypical world or did not have the personal skills to sustain a job for any length of time.

For years, people would look at the amazing things the students would make and say "You could sell these!" As early as 2010, when we first moved out of the barn and into the large warehouse, we tried to launch several small retail businesses either selling unique creations or making custom-built projects for customers. We could not successfully sustain these efforts as we did not have the resources, either material or staff, to

2010: Janet does late night touch-up

fully support the students and deliver the products. Every order became an intense and exhausting ordeal for our small staff, and most orders were finished by the two of us late at night. From a business perspective, paying staff to work with our students to produce goods for sale was extremely time consuming, which made it difficult to make a profit. At the time our entire program—staff time, space, materials—was paid for by parents. It became clear to us that this business model did not work.

NEVER SAY NEVER—AGAIN

Fast forward to January 2021. By then, staff time, space, and materials costs were completely covered by state funding, and most of our students also had Social Security income. A friend came to visit and tour the studio. He remarked, like so many others, that we should open a retail facility and give the students a place to sell their work. We started to offer our usual answers but stopped ourselves, HARD. This was a horse of a different color! Adding the state funded Autistry Comprehensive Adult Program had completely changed our business model.

Now, in this configuration, having the students designing, making, and selling things could become a meaningful activity, without being a huge expense. We started thinking about how we could do this. With Covid numbers soaring and the probable shutdown of in-person programs on the horizon, this seemed like a really bad time to pursue a new venture and expand our services. But a retail venture might potentially answer the question: what comes next?

Autistry was doing well under Covid restrictions even though we were still providing 100% remote service at the time. But we knew that eventually we would be back to in-person. To add the required activities, we would need more space. To launch a new facility would take additional funding, so the first step was to reach out to our major donors to see if they would support this venture. We asked them if this was a good idea or if they thought we were crazy. They responded, "You are crazy, and this is a good idea." The can of worms was open. It was time to fish.

We went online to search for a new space. A new property had just been listed: a 7,380 square foot retail space in downtown San Rafael with an existing coffee shop. The open space was reminiscent of the open warehouse—a blank canvas upon which we could paint our visions.

We encourage our students to take risks and to challenge themselves. Now it was time for us to do the same. We rolled up our

A new large empty space

sleeves and transformed the space. We portioned off the back part of the space to create a production workshop and training area. The front third of the building we left for a retail shop, and we planned to reopen the existing coffee shop.

What to call our new space? We wanted a name that reflected the Autistry mission to help individuals become more independent by developing fundamental skills: problem-solving, collaboration, critical thinking, and creativity. These skills are at the heart of the maker movement, a trend in academia and in the workplace to bring back hands-on learning. This movement is often called STEM (Science, Technology, Engineering, and Mathematics) or Project-Based Learning. Hands-on, experiential learning is what Autistry is all about. We named our new space Autistry Maker Incubator. This name embodies our guiding vision: we make makers.

CHANGING THE MINDSET

Autistry had begun with small Project-Based Therapy groups. These were very individualized sessions during which the clients created projects as a way to explore their personal issues and their identities. The projects were for them, by them, and, in many ways, reflections of them. We saw this new space as an opportunity to explore the creation of marketable products. This meant changing how the students viewed their work and the type of work they produced. We asked them to think about items that other people might want to purchase and that they could do as a group.

Retail venture: Makers Market

To consider what others might like or be interested in was a challenge for most of our students. A common issue for many autistics is the lack of "theory of mind," the social-cognitive skill that helps us interact with others by understanding their mental states—their hopes, interests, fears, and beliefs. Most of our students firmly believe that what they love to do, everyone loves to do. And what they are interested in, everyone is interested in.

One of the goals of the retail shop, which we named the Makers Market, is to get real-time, real-world feedback on student products. This feedback comes via written surveys or simply the evidence that some items do not sell. Based on the responses, we can make changes to the products and thereby provide an opportunity to experience the iterative process of production and overcome the Done is Good mentality. This is yet another place where we challenge our students to do better than their current best.

The initial production brainstorming meetings brought forth a raft of ideas, few of which would ever float: remake Thomas the Tank Engine and Friends videos, My Little Pony hand puppets, Power Ranger dioramas. We spent the first few meetings discussing copyright laws and breaking out of our creative comfort zones. Similar to the mode of thinking where one believes everyone loves what you love, we encountered the mindset that "I love this character so it is mine." We met with stiff resistance when we said that we could not sell products based on the characters created by other people. It was hard for many of the students to let go of creating clocks or puppets of their favorite characters and instead embrace their own unique visions. In the end, we had to set down a rule: no products based on copyrighted material. But with that avenue blocked off, the students uncovered a wealth of unique and individual ideas that were their very own.

PERFECTING THE PRODUCTS

When the excitement of endless possibilities narrowed down, we agreed on producing products that had individual creative input and could be replicated easily. Our first products were coaster sets. We chose to make them out of round, pre-cut, natural cork. These required using our laser cutter to etch original artwork onto the thick (2/5 inch), four inch diameter cork pieces.

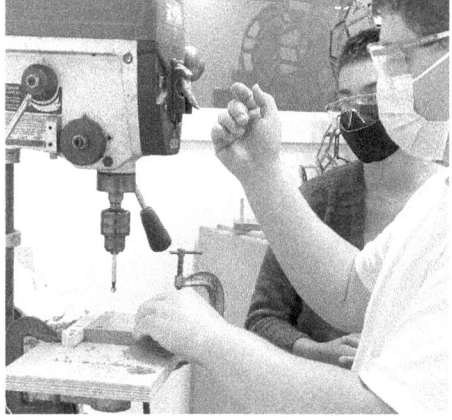

Drill press for making coaster bases

The coaster sets were the perfect first product for production. The design creation of the coasters and the bases to hold them provided the opportunity to develop many vocational skills with real world applications:

- Participating in design meetings to share ideas and get feedback from coworkers
- Creating a digital file for the laser cutter either from hand-drawn or computer-drawn images
- Creating a template to align the coaster accurately in the laser cutter
- Testing to find the correct laser cutter settings to produce the desired effect (and handling the frustration when the settings were wrong and burned the image rather than etching it)
- Measuring, cutting, and assembling the various wooden pieces for the coaster holders
- Packaging the etched coaster sets

Finding the right packaging for these sets was a great experience in iterative problem-solving. One of the requirements of the design was that the coasters would not end up spread across the shop floor. The students gathered around a table and brainstormed ideas from boxes to zip lock bags. They broke into small teams with each team creating a prototype of a chosen concept. The teams then presented their packaging solution to the whole group. The winning design was simple and elegant: a thin green ribbon wrapped around the entire set secured the cork coasters to the base.

Set of 6 coasters packaged, labeled, and signed

There was just one thing wrong with this design: only the top coaster was visible. You could no longer see the individual artwork of the

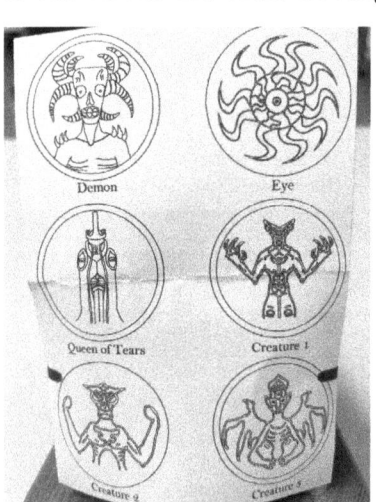

Now we can see what's inside the coaster package

other five coasters. The students did another round of brainstorming and arrived at a solution. They created a small folded label that on the front had the name of the coaster set, the artist's statement, artist's signature, and the Autistry logo. When unfolded, the label revealed all six individual designs. Problem solved.

The creation of the artwork itself provided constraints—must be unique, must be a set of six, must be a sketch that etched well into cork. Once the students accepted the constraints, they found they could create quite freely within them. The scoping and focus provided by the constraints also gave their work a cleaner, more professional look. The coasters were an immediate hit with our Autistry families and friends and will become a staple offering in the Autistry Makers Market.

OUT FOR A SPIN

The next product came about quite serendipitously. Geo, one of our production mentors, brought in a large set-up for doing spin art. Many of us remember spin art from summer camp crafts programs. The concept of spin art is to create colorful patterns by dropping paint onto a circular piece of wood and spinning it. The centrifugal force spreads the paint across the wooden

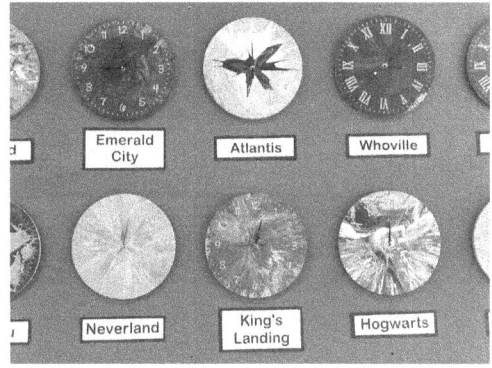

Unique and beautiful spin-art clocks

surface. This is a lovely and fun activity, but what could we make with this? The answer came in a flash: clocks.

Several students had already created clocks on the ShopBot based on their favorite cartoon or anime characters. These were for their per-

Geo helps a student adjust the clock hands

sonal use and generally hung in their bedrooms. For obvious copyright issues, these could not be sold in the retail shop. But spin art clocks are unique. By the very nature of their production each one is different. Spin art clocks became our next production project.

The production of the clocks offers opportunities for new skill acquisition: cutting the clock blanks, carving the numbers into the clock faces, and installing the hands and clockwork mechanisms. These tasks require planning, careful focus, and good fine motor control. The resulting clocks are beautiful, and they also keep good time!

PASSION FOR PUPPETS

Our third line of production evolved in a very Autistry way: starting small and progressing toward higher and higher quality. For Halloween the students made face masks. These were paper masks that they decorated with artwork, feathers, and various found objects. The masks were more like summer camp crafts projects than viable, marketable items. But they inspired us to make sock puppets.

Puppets encourage conversation

These simple sock puppets quickly became more and more sophisticated as students added fancy hats, teeth, and wildly expressive features. They also provided an opportunity for the students to learn to use the

Evolved project: elegant foam puppets

sewing machine. This skill came in handy as the sock puppets inspired us to create Muppet-style foam puppets. We experimented with several designs and construction methods. The mouths were a huge challenge as they gaped wide open when left on a stand. After many failed fixes, we came up with a spring mechanism that kept the mouth at a 45 degree angle—perfect.

The ideas continue to flow. Students come in every day with new project concepts. Working on the production ideas provides endless opportunities for creative exploration, design iteration, and problem-solving. We work together in small groups to build prototypes, then figure out the production process steps.

This experience has confirmed our commitment to project-based learning. We have seen how working on projects helps individuals overcome rigid thinking, how working together improves communication skills, and how pride in the finished product increases self-confidence.

Autistry—we make makers!

LISTENING TO, BUT NOT HEARING, TEMPLE GRANDIN

The Project-Based Therapy workshops and the Production Workshops have also taught us the importance of pushing ourselves to take that next step. We needed to challenge ourselves, our staff, and our students to take the risk of trying something new or making something good even better. That meant having enough respect for each other to provide what Temple Grandin calls the "loving push."

"Don't mollycoddle autistic kids," Temple Grandin often says. How many times have we sat in an audience with other parents, nodding our heads when she gives this advice? After she speaks, we applaud. We get our pictures taken with her and post them on the refrigerator and our Facebook page. We even get our children to pose with her and hope they will be as successful as she has been. But have we really heard what Temple Grandin is saying, and do we put her advice into practice?

The proponents of every program—special ed, vocational, social skills—will say they believe in a strengths-based, person-centered approach. They want to develop the talents and skills of the individual. However, we have seen too many programs that fail to have neurodivergent students take personal responsibility. Too many programs do not ever push students beyond their current limits, and too many programs do not help students persevere in the face of difficulty. We created Autistry because we found that whether autistic or neurotypical, it is imperative to wrestle with obstacles and overcome them.

We do our students no favors if we applaud a mediocre performance or achievement as if it were stellar. We believe in encouragement and positive reinforcement, but we also believe in a lifetime of raising the bar, of reaching higher. As we challenge our students (and ourselves), they rise to heights greater than we can imagine.

It is our role as teachers and mentors to hold high expectations for our students, to believe in their abilities, and to challenge them to take risks. Often we had to confront our own perceptions and assumptions. We had to let go of our doubts and our fears. We hesitated to put Ian in that first special day class because we worried he would be teased or mistreated. We also wrestled with our own emotions about being parents of an autistic son. To make Autistry work, and for it to work for Ian, we had to put all that aside and have faith that Ian could navigate his world, could stand up after falling down.

There is a popular saying in the disability community: the dignity of risk. We learned that we could not wrap our students in cotton wool, that by keeping them safe from all pain, we would be sending them a very clear message that we did not believe in their strengths or abilities.

Yep, autistics with power tools!

We would be robbing them of the dignity of overcoming obstacles—standing on their own two feet, using power tools, being independent.

The characteristics of autism make some aspects of life harder, but we never let them be an excuse to give up trying. One of the best lessons we have taught our students is how to problem solve given their personal constraints. Our experience has been that each person has different strengths and weaknesses, so each of our solutions will be different. Typical pathways and tool sets may not work for autistic individuals. But that just challenges us to find alternative ways to accomplish goals.

THE ONE LESS TRAVELED BY

Fifteen years have passed since our first workshop in the barn. We have worked with hundreds of individuals, each of whom taught us something new about neurodiversity and about ourselves. We learned to listen to unspoken communications and to view the world from new angles. The students taught us that not only beauty, but reality is in the eye of the beholder. To truly understand our students and to connect with them we needed to enter their worlds. And what wonderful, rich, and amazing worlds they are.

The two of us began our adult lives traveling along very different career paths. At first, the backyard build stuff workshops seemed like a temporary detour, and we thought we would return to our mainstream careers. But working with the autistic students soon became the main highway.

Our journey to create Autistry has challenged us, surprised us, and given us much joy. We are honored to share this journey, share this road with our students.

Yeah, but we aren't done yet!

Core Value #12: Accept that each person lives their own reality.

CORE VALUES THAT KEEP US ON TRACK

Listen to what experience teaches.

Be flexible and do what works for the client.

Neurological differences may define us, but they need not limit us.

Share your passion and be willing to learn.

Explore project ideas with no judgment while
holding project production to a high standard.

Stay focused on what works, not what gets funded.

Respect and support the many aspects of independence.

Never stop learning.

Healthy living involves the body and the brain.

Partner with organizations with a strong community
mission and range of skill-building opportunities.

Staying safe does not rule out creative growth.

Accept that each person lives their own reality.

ACKNOWLEDGEMENTS

There are many people to thank for helping us translate our experiences into a book. **Cynthia Gregory**, our editor and writing coach, provided much-appreciated advice and encouragement. **Courtney Flavin**, our eagle-eyed copy editor, kept our commas straight and our words flowing. **Suzi Schell** worked tirelessly to create the layout and cover design and never complained about our endless revisions. Sisters **Karyn Lawson** and **Stacy Jardine** were always just a phone call away and ready to lift our spirits when needed. **Phil Lewis**, an Autistry mentor, read early versions and gave honest, thoughtful feedback. Our board of directors, **Cliff Saron**, **Barbara Waite**, **Gordon Lithgow**, **Gail Theller**, and **Laura Hess**, supported us all along the way with positive encouragement.

And a special thank you to **Rafael Altman** and the **Jonathan and Kathleen Altman Foundation** who years ago saw the value of our work, believed in us, and supported us.

The writing process took many hours out of our workdays, and those hours would not have been possible without the tremendous support of our senior Autistry staff. **Sara Gardner** expanded her workload to include client onboarding. **Rhoda Robertson** took on many of the complex administrative chores that we were unable to address. **Shelby Green** added bookkeeping to her long list of tasks. **Benji Harrington** and **Tim Flavin** made sure that all the students were engaged in meaningful projects and activities. We want you all to know that we noticed and that we truly value your contributions this last year of writing. We couldn't have done this without you.

Our deepest gratitude is to our students and mentors—past and present. We love your creative projects, quirky ideas, and unique perspectives. We have learned so much from all of you over these last fifteen years. Together we are building something special.

NOTES

CHAPTER 1:

Pg. 2: There are many wonderful quotes from Meryl Streep discussing acting and her long career. This one I found here: actingmagazine.com/2023/03/11-inspirational-quotes-by-meryl-streep/

Pg. 3: Grandin, Temple, *Thinking in Pictures* (New York: Doubleday, 1995). One of the first books written by an autistic about autism. This was the book that convinced Dan that he is autistic.

Pg 7: Kanner, Leo, *Autistic Disturbances of Affective Contact, Nervous Child, Vol 2* (1943), pp.217-250. Available at: http://simonsfoundation.s3.amazonaws.com/share/071207-leo-kanner-autistic-affective-contact.pdf [Accessed March 8, 2023]. Kanner suggested in this article that autism might be caused by cold, unemotional mothers. This concept dubbed the Refrigerator Mom was championed by Bruno Bettelheim who in the 1940s was the director of the Orthogenic School for Troubled Children at the University of Chicago.

CHAPTER 2:

Pg. 38: Iris Murdoch. Retrieved March 9, 2023, from AZQuotes.com Web site: www.azquotes.com/quote/377145 This is a quote that hangs above our workstations to remind us not to seek perfection.

CHAPTER 3:

Pg. 42: Grandin, Temple, and Debra Moore, *The Loving Push: How Parents and Professionals Can Help Spectrum Kids Become Successful Adults* (Arlington, Texas: Future Horizons, 2016.

CHAPTER 4:

Pg. 56: Tobin, Martin J., *Mentoring: Seven Roles and Some Specifics*, American Journal of Respiratory and Critical Care Medicine, 170 (02) pp. 114-117 (2004).

CHAPTER 5:

Pg. 64: Heimann, Jim, *California Crazy and Beyond: Roadside Vernacular Architecture* (San Francisco: Chronicle Books, 2001. This is one of Ian's favorite books. It has always stimulated his imagination and we still look through it when designing dioramas.

Pg. 67: Those interested in finding out more about John Allen's TimeSave should check out gdlines.org/GDLines/Timesaver.html.

CHAPTER 6:

Pg. 73: Dr. Bryna Siegel is the author of many books on autism. She is also the founder of the Autism Center of Northern California (www. acnc.org).

Pg. 73: The ShopBot is an amazing piece of equipment and very safe for use by just about anybody. To learn more see: www.shopbottools.com.

Pg. 78: Dedication to Special Education is a great example of what can be done when parents come together. One of the issues we recognized when we first met together in 1997 was that our children, with their various learning challenges and support needs, are expensive to teach. And because of that, they were often left behind. So we set about to raise money so that every school in Marin County could support our children. Over the years, DSE has raised nearly $2,000,000. In 2008, DSE began a grant-giving program for teachers to apply for resources they need. Well over $1,000,000 has been put into the classrooms. Check out DSE: www.specialed. org.

CHAPTER 7:

Pg. 87: The Independent Living Skills Assessment Tool created by the Washington State Department of Social and Health Services has been refined and developed by many organizations since it first appeared in 2000. It is still a useful assessment tool and can be used as a foundation for creating assessments tailored to reflect the issues facing individuals in specific communities.

The fifteen original categories were:
1. Money Management/Consumer Awareness
2. Food Management
3. Personal Appearance and Hygiene
4. Health
5. Housekeeping
6. Housing
7. Transportation
8. Educational Planning
9. Job Seeking Skills
10. Job Maintenance Skills
11. Emergency and Safety Skills
12. Knowledge of Community Resources
13. Interpersonal Skills
14. Legal Skills
15. Pregnancy Prevention/Parenting and Child Care

CHAPTER 8:

Pg. 98: Grandin, Temple, and Betsy Lerner. *Visual Thinking: The Hidden Gifts of People Who Think in Pictures, Patterns, and Abstractions* (New York: Riverhead Books, 2022). A well-researched and yet personal book on the unique way neurodiverse individuals view the world and the many ways their perspectives can and do impact the world.

Pg. 104: Morrison, Grant: *Supergods: What Masked Vigilantes, Miraculous Mutants, and a Sun God from Smallville Can Teach Us About Being Human.*

Pg: 104: The Pixar Story Xperiential is developing rapidly. You can learn more on their website: www.storyxperiential.com.

CHAPTER 9:

Pg. 115: More information about The Driver Rehabilitation Institute founded by   Dr. Miriam Monahan is available on their website: www. driverrehabinstitute.org.

Pg. 123: A good starting point for exploring the gut-brain connection: www.health.harvard.edu/diseases-and-conditions/the-gut-brain-connection.

CHAPTER 10:

Pg. 129: The Western Railway Museum is located at 5848 State Highway 12, Suisun City, CA. It is open Saturdays and Sundays year-round. For more information, see: www.wrm.org.

Pg. 132: The stables and offices of Square Peg Foundation are located in Half Moon Bay, CA. This is a tremendous organization that is helping the neurodiverse population and saving the lives of retired racehorses. For more information, see: www.squarepegfoundation.org.

Pg. 139: The 39 county parks are an important part of life in Marin. They provide homes to a wide variety of fauna and flora and endless enjoyment to human inhabitants. For more information, see: www.parks.marincounty.org.

CHAPTER 11:

Pg.143: Each year the Center for Volunteer & Nonprofit Leadership presents the Heart of Marin Awards to nonprofit organizations in Marin County. For more information, see www.cvnl.org/heart-of-marin.

For more information about the San Francisco Bay Area Jefferson Awards, see: www.cbsnews.com/sanfrancisco/jefferson-awards.

CHAPTER 12:

For more information about Autistry Studios, see: www.autistry.com.

THE AUTHORS

JANET LAWSON

Janet Lawson is a psychotherapist with a background in film and theater. In addition to her B.A. degree in Film Studies from UC Berkeley and an MS degree in Counseling Psychology from Dominican University, Janet has an MS in Library and Information Science from Indiana University. She brings all her skills and experience to work as she continues to develop Autistry Studios, a therapeutic makerspace for autistic teens and adults. Janet is the mother of an autistic son.

DAN SWEARINGEN

Dan Swearingen is the parent of an autistic child and a Mentor/Maker/Nonprofit Administrator in San Rafael, California. Dan has an MS in Physics from Cal. State Northridge and an MA in Astronomy from Indiana University. Dan worked for many years in the San Francisco Bay Area as a programmer and manager of programmers before he co-founded Autistry Studios in 2008.

.